Waterfront Homes

200

PLANS FOR RIVER, LAKE OR SEA

HOME PLANNERS, LLC
Wholly owned by Hanley-Wood, LLC
TUCSON, ARIZONA

Waterfront Homes

Published by Home Planners, LLC
Wholly owned by Hanley-Wood, LLC
Editorial and Corporate Offices:
3275 West Ina Road, Suite 110
Tucson, Arizona 85741

Distribution Center:
29333 Lorie Lane
Wixom, Michigan 48393

Rickard D. Bailey, *CEO and Publisher*
Cindy Coatsworth Lewis, *Director of Publishing*
Jan Prideaux, *Senior Editor*
Marian E. Haggard, *Editor*
Chester E. Hawkins, *Graphic Designer*
Front cover design by Jay C. Walsh

Design/Photography Credits
Front Cover: Design Q435 by Select Home Designs
                     Photo by Bri-Mar Photography,
                     Brian Gill Photographer

Back Cover: Plan 9757 by Donald A. Gardner Architects, Inc.
                     Photos by Riley & Riley Photography, Inc.

Book design by Chester E. Hawkins

First Printing, September 1999

10 9 8 7 6 5 4 3

Printed in the United States of America

Library of Congress Catalog Card Number: 99-073461

ISBN softcover: 1-881955-64-8

Table — of Contents

LARRY E. BELK DESIGNS
Through the years, Larry E. Belk has worked with individuals and builders alike to provide a quality product. Flowing, open spaces and interesting angles define his interiors. Great emphasis is placed on providing views that showcase the natural environment.

LARRY W. GARNETT & ASSOCIATES, INC.
Starting as a designer of homes for Houston-area residents, Garnett & Associates has been marketing designs nationally for the past ten years. A well-respected design firm, the company's plans are regularly featured in *House Beautiful, Country Living, Home* and *Professional Builder.*

HOME PLANNERS
Headquartered in Tucson, Arizona, with additional offices in Detroit, Home Planners is one of the longest-running and most successful home design firms in the United States. With over 2,500 designs in its portfolio, the company provides a wide range of styles, sizes and types of homes for the residential builder.

DONALD A. GARDNER ARCHITECTS, INC.
The South Carolina firm of Donald A. Gardner was established in response to a growing demand for residential designs that reflect constantly changing lifestyles. The company's specialty is providing homes with refined, custom-style details and unique features, such as passive-solar designs and open floor plans.

SELECT HOME DESIGNS
Select Home Designs has 50 years of experience delivering top-quality and affordable residential designs to the North American housing market. Since the company's inception in 1948, more than 350,000 new homes throughout North America and overseas have been built from Select's plans. Select's design team is constantly striving to develop the best new plans for today's lifestyles.

UNITED DESIGN ASSOCIATES, INC.
United Design offers award-winning Ideal Home Plans to builders and consumers worldwide. "At United Design, we know you've got a lot more to think about than plans, so we make it simple. First and foremost, we design beautiful, intelligent homes that appeal to clients of all interests."

CHATHAM HOME PLANNING, INC.
Chatham Home Planning, Inc. is a professional member of the AIBD and a member of the National Home Builder's Association. Robert Chatham founded the company over fifteen years ago, and now has approximately 15,000 plans in stock. The company specializes in designs that have a strong historical look: Early American Southern cottages, Georgian classics, French Colonials, Southern Louisiana designs, traditionals and country cottages.

PERFECT HOME PLANS
Samuel Paul and David J. Paul, a father and son team of architects, have established an outstanding reputation in the design of single family homes. Perfect Home Plans was founded in the early 1950s and David Paul joined the company in 1963. The firm has received professional awards for outstanding design from the Architectural Record, New York Chapter of The American Institute of Architects and the Long Island Association of Commerce and Industry.

THE SATER DESIGN COLLECTION
The Sater Design Collection has a long established tradition of providing South Florida's most diverse and extraordinary custom designed homes. This is exemplified by over 50 national design awards, numerous magazine features and, most important, satisfied clients.

STEPHEN FULLER
Stephen S. Fuller established his design group with the tenets of innovation, quality, originality and uncompromising architectural techniques in traditional and European homes. Especially popular throughout the Southeast, Stephen Fullers' plans are known for their extensive detail and thoughtful design.

ALAN MASCORD DESIGN ASSOCIATES, INC.
Founded in 1983 as a local supplier to the building community, Mascord Design Associates of Portland, Oregon began to successfully publish plans nationally in 1985. The company's trademark is creating floor plans that work well and exhibit excellent traffic patterns.

THE HOUSING ASSOCIATES
Rodney L. Pfotenhauer opened the doors of The Housing Associates in 1987 as a design consultant and illustrator for the manufactured housing industry. Almost from the beginning, his efforts caught the attention of the public. Pfotenhauer's designs are characterized by carefully composed traditional exteriors with up-to-date interiors.

LIVING CONCEPTS HOME PLANNING
With more than twenty years of design experience, Living Concepts Home Planning has built an outstanding reputation for its many award-winning residential designs. Based in Charlotte, North Carolina, the company was founded by partners Frank Snodgrass, Chris Boush, Kim Bunting and Derik Boush. Because of its affinity for glass and designs that take full advantage of outside views, Living Concepts specializes in homes for golf and lakefront communities.

DRUMMOND DESIGNS, INC.
Drummond Designs has been involved in the business of residential architecture since 1973, with over 70,000 satisfied customers. They have achieved this by keeping up with the trends, and sometimes creating them. Their primary goal is to offer consumers top-quality homes that meet or exceed most of the world's building code requirements.

NELSON DESIGN GROUP
Michael E. Nelson is a certified member of the American Institute of Building Designers, providing both custom and stock residential home plans. He designs homes that families enjoy now and which also bring maximum appraisal value at resale. His travels have kept him on the cutting edge of the design market and updated as to new building industry applications.

ANDY MCDONALD DESIGN GROUP
Andy McDonald, CPBD, is a residential designer whose scrupulous regard for scale, balance and historical detailing has earned him a stellar reputation. As a result of his national recognition, Andy has been commissioned to design entire communities, as well as style-coordinated parcels in upscale developments. Of particular appeal to McDonald are the classic designs of Old World France, Spain and England.

on the Waterfront

...an Introduction to Living by the Water

by Marian E. Haggard

The babbling of a nearby stream, the cry of shore-birds in the morning, the gentle lap of waves breaking along the beach—these natural treasures evoke happy, peaceful days.

As the pace of living speeds up, it becomes more essential for people to create a more harmonious and tranquil home environment. Waterfront living offers you the opportunity to experience the magic of living by the water, surrounded by the beautiful signs and sounds of nature. With one of the designs in this book as your beginning, you can create the home base to enjoy a quiet stroll along the water's edge, boating or waterskiing at your doorstep, beach-combing after a storm or just relaxing on your deck and enjoying the spectacular scenery.

In this marvelous collection of homes, we have divided up the waterways into five definitive sections, providing a glimpse of the particular architecture true to different needs. A waterfront home has many moods: lightfilled, stormy, breezy, serene—and equally comfortable to be shared with guests or solitude.

For riverside living, homes with traditional fronts or narrow footprints show off their versatility by offering a plentitude of windows and outdoor gathering spots toward the rear of the home—perfect for relaxing and watching the sunset cast its golden reflection on the gently rippling water. Some homes are designed to face the water, offering a side or the rear of the home to the street, as in Design 9630 on page 65.

Above: Design A169, page 18

Above: Design A302, page 23   Right: Design 9661, page 12

Many of these homes feature crawlspace foundations instead of extensive basements, perfect for high water tables. Those with basements are designed with walk-out capability or plenty of space for storage. For a European flavor, turn to Design M506 on page 41, where you'll observe French and English cottages rubbing elbows with Northwest rustic styles.

In *Seashore Silhouettes,* beginning on page 75, the feeling of a calm ocean breeze reaches right out of the book, gently refreshing you and introducing a variety of designs perfect for residing near the ocean. Here you'll browse styles ranging from simple Floridian bungalows with large covered porches (as seen in Design 6691 on page 101), to Northwest Rustics—just right for a

rocky coastline (as exemplified by design V004 on page 103). These enchanting homes offer such amenities as covered porches—perfect for whale watching—multi-story windows to maximize lavish views, and a few with observation (or lookout) lofts. There are tropical styles, at home in the Florida Keys, and sturdy homes perfect for enjoying an ocean view.

Next is a chapter that invites you to meander down to the lake. Here, multi-level homes take center stage, with various levels offering balconies and patios from which to watch the sun ripple on the water, or to share a child's triumph as they learn how to water ski. Lakefront homes can range from a small, cozy cottage like Design F100 on page 108—perfect for a weekend getaway or empty-

nester—to the lavish three-level home found on page 131 (Design 4308). With everything from traditional, slightly formal brick exteriors to more European-flavored stucco, the variety of possibilities will convince everyone that their favorite design is just right for living near the lake.

In **Up On Stilts** (starting on page 147), pier foundations make a stand. Elevated for living really close to the water, these homes are not just for the seashore. Check out Design Z117 on page 149 and think of the storage possibilities. Or, if you really like your privacy, Design Y044 on page 164, with its very separate master suite, will definitely please you. Traditionals, Floridians and bungalows fill these pages, proving that variety is the spice of life.

And last but not least, **Barefoot Luxury**, beginning on page 173, provides the icing on the cake, with lavish designs such as Q435 on page 178 and more subtly luxurious homes such as Design 2937 on page 193. Here, it's not necessarily size that is the luxury, but the abundance of amenities. Wet bars, guest suites, deluxe master bedroom suites, recreation rooms and indoor pools all combine to pamper the lucky owners and provide excellent backdrops to waterfront living.

Whether your dream is a home by the sea, lake or river, you will be pleasantly surprised at the variety available from which to choose. So relax, curl up with this book, choose your perfect waterfront home—and begin to live your dream of peaceful days with gentle breezes!

Design Z098, page 126

Beachcomber's

On a hot

summer's day,

wander you might—

Down where

water meets land

under golden

sunlight.

Treasures there

abound,

just waiting to be

found,

To add to the

searcher's delight!

—MEH

Any time you walk along the shore, whether it's the seashore, lakeshore or riverside, there are fun and interesting things to find. Almost everybody has picked up shells, driftwood and other small (and some not so small!) objects from the beach at one time or another. The types and numbers of organisms will vary with the weather, tides (if there are any) and numbers of passersby. And each beach will offer different treasures.

Before You Go:
Gathering a few tools to take with you will make your stroll upon the beach both more interesting and more convenient. A small pail, a garden trowel, a putty knife and a magnifying glass, while not necessary, can be useful.

Beachcombing Techniques:
* Go slowly, be patient and look carefully
* Dig into the sand and mud and investigate the water's edge
* Leave organisms in their natural habitat since most can't survive outside their marine environment
* When handling organisms, be careful and be gentle
* Be moderate in the nonliving shells and organisms you take home

SANDY BEACHES
Beachcombing along the seashore gives good results almost all the time, due to the tides. However, virtually every beach can be productive at one time or another, especially after a storm. Using a rake or small putty knife just before or after low tide, you may be able to find many of the species that live buried in the sand. You may also find buried shells by recognizing the tracks they leave on the surface.

Things you might find:
- ☑ Conch shells
- ☑ Moon shells
- ☑ Tulip shells
- ☑ Purple Dwarf Olive shells
- ☑ Bottles buried in the sand
- ☑ Drift Wood
- ☑ Coral (near oceans)
- ☑ Jellyfish (careful!)
- ☑ Sand Dollar shells
- ☑ Horseshoe Crabs

Checklist

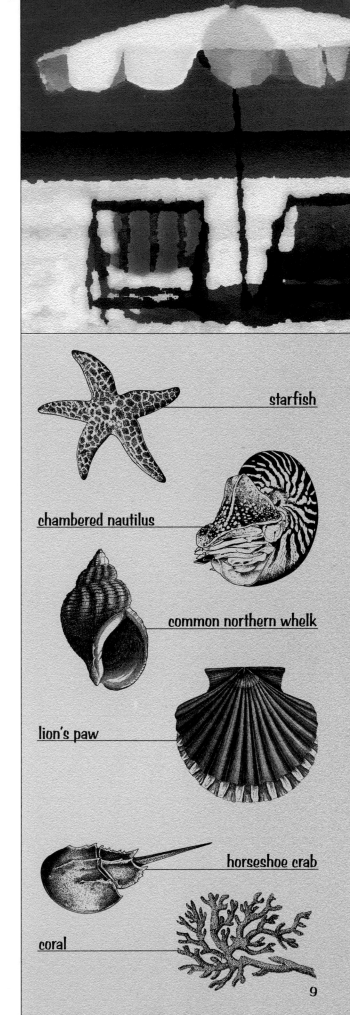

MUD FLATS

Both marine mud flats and those along the riverside can produce a number of shells, organisms and flotsam. Rivers are very good at changing the scenery around them, and will bury and reveal a variety of interesting items. Again, the use of a rake or trowel will be handy to dig after burrowing bivalved shells. A word of warning however, mud can be a deadly trap and it is advisable to find out about the site and the tides (if there are any).

Things you might find:
- ☑ Giant Western Nassa shells
- ☑ Eastern Mud Snails
- ☑ Clams
- ☑ Crawfish
- ☑ Fishing lures
- ☑ Waterworn wood
- ☑ Bottles
- ☑ Toys

ROCKY BEACHES

While sand and mud is better suited for some shells and for the majority of flotsam, rocky beaches are often the home to many gastropod species (specifically shaped shells). Tools for searching would be different here, with a steel bar or a stout stick, as standard equipment for hunting shells. This would be useful for moving small rocks to see what's lurking beneath them. Remember to peek into all the pools, small caves and niches. Don't forget to look under rocks too. Be cautious however. Rocky beaches can be dangerous. Some rocks are slippery even without a covering of water, so remember to move slowly and carefully. If there are tides in the area, know whether they are going out or coming in so you don't get trapped.

Things you might find:
- ☑ Red Abalone shells
- ☑ Bleeding Tooth shells
- ☑ Periwinkles
- ☑ Three-winged Murex shells
- ☑ Dog Winkle shells
- ☑ Rockweed
- ☑ Asterid Sea Stars
- ☑ Hermit Crabs
- ☑ Rock Crabs

So when you go wandering on a beach, don't forget a pail to hold your treasures, and your sunscreen to prevent a sunburn, but the main thing to remember whenever you go beachcombing is... HAVE FUN!!

starfish

chambered nautilus

common northern whelk

lion's paw

horseshoe crab

coral

Design
3699
LD

First Floor:
1,356 sq. ft.

Second Floor:
490 sq. ft.

Total:
1,846 sq. ft.

Width:
50'-7"

Depth:
38'-0"

Photo by Andrew D. Lautman

This home, as shown in the photograph, may differ from the actual blueprints. For more detailed information, please check the floor plans carefully.

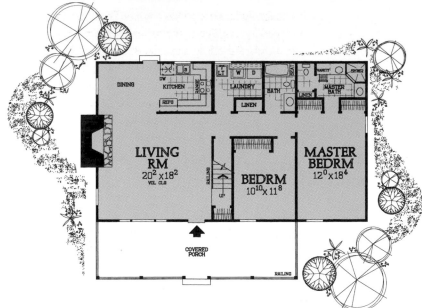

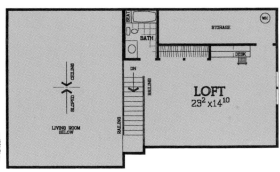

QUOTE ONE®
Cost to build? See page 198 to order complete cost estimate to build this house in your area!

Split-log siding and a rustic balustrade create country charm with this farmhouse-style retreat—perfect for river- or lakeside living. An open living area features a natural stone fireplace and a cathedral ceiling with exposed rough-sawn beams and brackets. A generous kitchen and dining area complement the living room and share the warmth of its fireplace. A master bedroom with complete bath, and a nearby family bedroom with hall bath, complete the main floor. Upstairs, a spacious loft affords extra sleeping space—or provides a hobby/recreation area—and offers a full bath.

Design by
©Home Planners

Design 3331

L

First Floor:
1,115 sq. ft.

Second Floor:
690 sq. ft.

Total:
1,805 sq. ft.

Width:
43'-0"

Depth:
32'-0"

This quaint Tudor cottage has an open floor plan that is designed for easy living. The gathering room is accented with a cathedral ceiling and a full Palladian window. The dining room is joined to the efficient kitchen with extra entertaining space available on the deck. The first-floor master suite features a large compartmented bath and bumped-out windows. Upstairs, a lounge overlooks the gathering room. Two additional bedrooms and a full hall bath complete the second floor.

Rear View

This home, as shown in the photograph, may differ from the actual blueprints. For more detailed information, please check the floor plans carefully.

Design by
© **Home Planners**

QUOTE ONE®
Cost to build? See page 198
to order complete cost estimate
to build this house in your area!

BEDROOM
16⁴ x 10⁶

ATTIC ACCESS

BATH   ATTIC

BEDROOM
11⁰ x 10⁶

LOUNGE
11⁰ x 17⁰

UPPER
GATHERING RM

BALCONY

BATH

LINEN LINEN

DINING
10¹⁰ x 11⁶

DECK

KITCHEN
9⁰ x 12⁶

GATHERING RM
15⁴ x 15⁰

MASTER
BEDROOM
11⁴ x 16⁶

FOYER

COVERED PORCH

Design 9661

First Floor:
1,416 sq. ft.

Second Floor:
445 sq. ft.

Total:
1,861 sq. ft.

Bonus Room:
284 sq. ft.

Width:
58'-3"

Depth:
68'-9"

Photos by Riley & Riley
Photography, Inc.

An arched entrance and windows provide a touch of class to the exterior of this plan. The dining room displays round columns at the entrance while the great room boasts a cathedral ceiling, fireplace and arched window over exterior doors to the deck, where sunsets and cool breezes can be enjoyed. The large kitchen opens to the breakfast nook, and sliding glass doors present a second access to the deck. In the master suite is a walk-in closet and lavish bath. On the second level are two bedrooms and a full bath. Please specify basement or crawlspace foundation when ordering.

Rear View

This home, as shown in the photographs, may differ from the actual blueprints. For more detailed information, please check the floor plans carefully.

DECK

seat

spa

arched window above door

GREAT RM.
15-4 × 18-0
(cathedral ceiling)

fireplace

KIT./BRKFST.
16-8 × 16-0

master bath

walk-in closet

walk-in closet

pd. rm.

up

sto.

MASTER BED RM.
13-0 × 13-6

FOYER
7-8 × 9-0

DINING
12-4 × 12-4

UTILITY
10-0 × 6-4

w

d

up

storage

PORCH

GARAGE
20-0 × 20-0

© 1991 Donald A. Gardner Architects, Inc.

BED RM.
10-4 × 11-9

walk-in closet

down

bath

cl

BED RM.
12-4 × 13-6

down

BONUS RM.
11-0 × 20-0

QUOTE ONE®
Cost to build? See page 198
to order complete cost estimate
to build this house in your area!

Design by
Donald A. Gardner Architects, Inc.

Photos by Riley & Riley Photography, Inc.

Design
9757

First Floor:
1,715 sq. ft.

Second Floor:
620 sq. ft.

Total:
2,335 sq. ft.

Bonus Room:
265 sq. ft.

Width:
58'-6"

Depth:
50'-3"

Rear View

This home, as shown in the photographs, may differ from the actual blueprints. For more detailed information, please check the floor plans carefully.

With a decided Traditional flavor, this two-story home features country living at its best. The foyer opens to a study or living room on the left. The dining room on the right offers large proportions and full windows with a view of the lake. The family room remains open to the kitchen and breakfast room. Here, sunny meals are guaranteed with a bay window overlooking the rear yard. In the master suite, a bayed sitting area, a walk-in closet and a pampering bath are sure to please. Upstairs, two bedrooms flank a loft or study area and a full hall bath.

QUOTE ONE®

Cost to build? See page 198 to order complete cost estimate to build this house in your area!

Design by
Donald A. Gardner Architects, Inc.

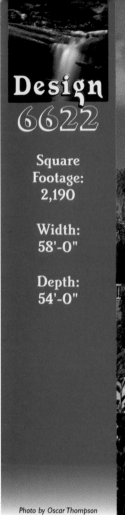

Design
6622

Square Footage:
2,190

Width:
58'-0"

Depth:
54'-0"

Photo by Oscar Thompson

This home, as shown in the photograph, may differ from the actual blueprints. For more detailed information, please check the floor plans carefully.

A strikingly simple staircase leads to the dramatic entry of this contemporary design. The foyer opens to an expansive grand room with a fireplace and a built-in entertainment center. An expansive lanai opens from the living area and offers good inside/outside relationships. For more traditional occasions and planned events, a front-facing dining room offers a place for quiet, elegant entertaining. The master suite features a lavish bath with two sizable walk-in closets, a windowed whirlpool tub, twin lavatories and a compartmented toilet. Double doors open from the gallery hall to a secluded study that is convenient to the master bedroom. Two additional bedrooms share a private hall and a full bath on the opposite side of the plan.

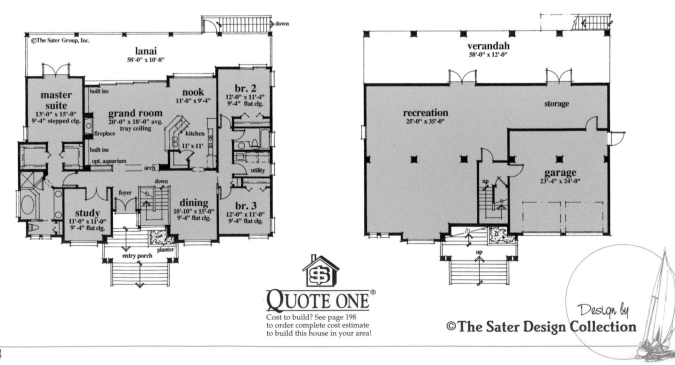

QUOTE ONE®

Cost to build? See page 198 to order complete cost estimate to build this house in your area!

©The Sater Design Collection

Design by

Design
6620

Main Level:
2,066 sq. ft.

Upper Level:
810 sq. ft.

Total:
2,876 sq. ft.

Lower Level:
1,260 sq. ft.

Width:
64'-0"

Depth:
45'-0"

This home, as shown in the photograph, may differ from the actual blueprints. For more detailed information, please check the floor plans carefully.

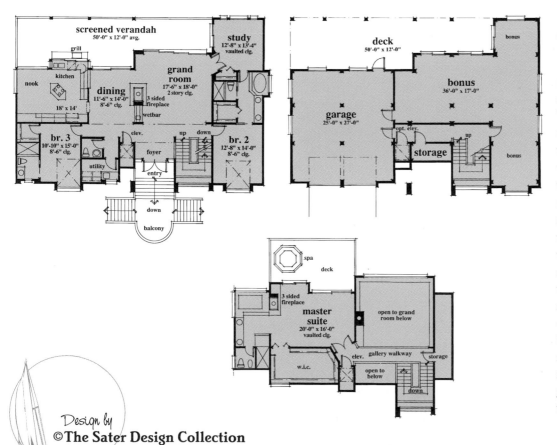

This striking Floridian plan is designed for entertaining. A large, open floor plan offers soaring, sparkling space for planned gatherings. The foyer leads to the grand room, highlighted by a glass fireplace, a wet bar and wide views of the outdoors. Both the grand room and the formal dining room open to a screened veranda. The first floor includes two spacious family bedrooms and a secluded study that opens from the grand room. The second-floor master suite offers sumptuous amenities, including a private deck and spa, a three-sided fireplace, a sizable walk-in closet and a gallery hall with an overlook to the grand room.

Design by
©The Sater Design Collection

First Floor:
1,122 sq. ft.

Second Floor:
528 sq. ft.

Total:
1,650 sq. ft.

Width:
34'-0"

Depth:
52'-5"

Photo by Chris A. Little of Atlanta

This home, as shown in the photograph, may differ from the actual blueprints.
For more detailed information, please check the floor plans carefully.

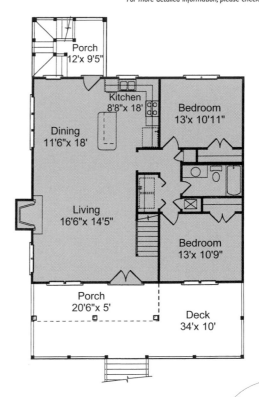

Bedroom
14'x 11'2"

Master
Bedroom
13'x 13'6"

Open to
Below

Porch
12'x 9'5"

Kitchen
8'8"x 18'

Dining
11'6"x 18'

Bedroom
13'x 10'11"

Living
16'6"x 14'5"

Bedroom
13'x 10'9"

Porch
20'6"x 5'

Deck
34'x 10'

This waterfront retreat is set up off the ground with a pier foundation, providing outstanding views from all sides. Two first-floor
bedrooms share access to the full bath and laundry closet. Great
views and plenty of closet space enhance both bedrooms. Upstairs,
another family bedroom is brightened with a view of the living area
below and outside the vistas. The master bedroom features a dormer
window, a walk-in closet, private vanity and a shared, compartmented
bath with a bumped-out tub accented by a pleasant window view.

©Chatham Home Planning, Inc.

Design by

Design
4559

First Floor:
507 sq. ft.

Second Floor:
438 sq. ft.

Total:
945 sq. ft.

Width:
26'-0"

Depth:
20'-0"

This home, as shown in the photograph, may differ from the actual blueprints.
For more detailed information, please check the floor plans carefully.

ombine a shingled exterior and an upstairs deck, and you can recall the joy of seaside vacations. Let breezes ruffle your hair and ocean spray settle on your skin in this comfortable two-story home. Unique window treatments provide views from every room. The lifestyle is casual, including meals prepared in a kitchen separated from the living room by a snack-bar counter. A powder room and a wet bar complete the upstairs. The first floor houses two bedrooms, a full bath and a laundry room. Built-ins make the most of compact space.

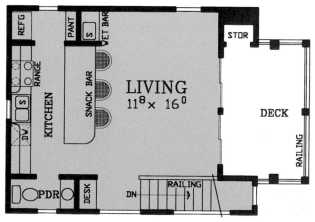

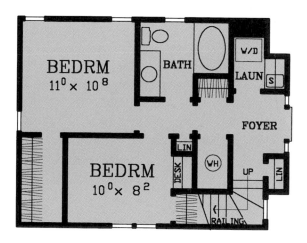

Design by
©**Home Planners**

17

Design
A169

First Floor:
2,414 sq. ft.

Second Floor:
1,543 sq. ft.

Total:
3,957 sq. ft.

Bonus Room:
544 sq. ft.

Width:
70'-4"

Depth:
88'-6"

Photo by Living Concepts

This home, as shown in the photograph, may differ from the actual blueprints.
For more detailed information, please check the floor plans carefully.

This lovely stone house with its gracious covered porch and balustrade offers fine European detailing and a very up-to-date interior. An island work area, a walk-in pantry and plenty of counter space make the modern kitchen a pleasant place for the cook, who can feel a part of activities in the breakfast area and the family room. The rear veranda is reached from the laundry room, the formal dining room and the master bedroom. The master bath features a walk-in closet, a compartmented toilet, dual lavatories and a corner tub. A nearby living room could also serve as a guest bedroom. The second floor offers three bedrooms, "Captain's quarters" (a room with many possibilities) and a bonus area over the garage.

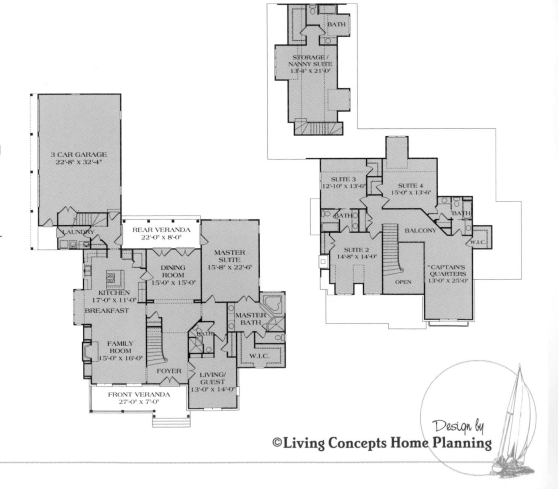

©Living Concepts Home Planning

Design by

18

Design A287

First Floor:
2,660 sq. ft.

Second Floor:
914 sq. ft.

Total:
3,574 sq. ft.

Guest Lodging:
733 sq. ft.

Width:
114'-8"

Depth:
75'-10"

Photo by Living Concepts

This home, as shown in the photograph, may differ from the actual blueprints.
For more detailed information, please check the floor plans carefully.

Gently curved arches and dormers contrast with the straight lines of gables and wooden columns on this French-style stone exterior. Small paned windows are enhanced by shutters; tall chimneys and a cupola add height. Inside, a spacious gathering room, with an impressive fireplace, opens to a cheery morning room. The delightful kitchen includes a beam ceiling, a triangular work island, a walk-in pantry and an angular counter with a snack bar. The nearby laundry provides a sink, a good-sized work area and plenty of room for storage. The first-floor master suite boasts a bay-windowed sitting nook, a deluxe bath and a handy study. The second floor includes a balcony overlooking the gathering room, two bedroom suites and a large guest area over the garage.

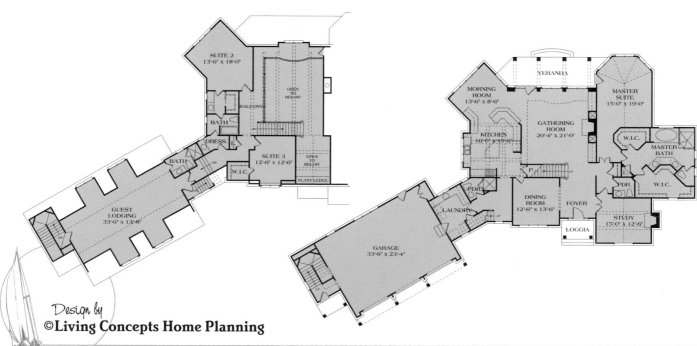

Design by
©Living Concepts Home Planning

Design
A213

First Floor:
1,729 sq. ft.

Second Floor:
2,312 sq. ft.

Total:
4,041 sq. ft.

Bonus Space:
800 sq. ft.

Width:
71'-6"

Depth:
60'-0"

This home, as shown in the photograph, may differ from the actual blueprints.
For more detailed information, please check the floor plans carefully.

Entertaining will be a breeze for the owners of this imposing French manor house. Formal rooms are directly off the foyer, with a powder room nearby. Family members and friends may prefer the beam-ceilinged gathering room, with its fireplace and access from the covered front terrace. The kitchen, which easily serves both areas, features a walk-in pantry, an island cooktop and a large breakfast nook. Upstairs, the master suite contains a sitting room and access to a private balcony, as well as a sumptuous bath. A reading area is centrally located to all four bedrooms, and a recreation room adds another opportunity for relaxation.

Design by
©**Living Concepts Home Planning**

Design
A181

First Floor:
4,151 sq. ft.

Second Floor:
3,081 sq. ft.

Total:
7,232 sq. ft.

Apartment:
873 sq. ft.

Pool House:
1,280 sq. ft.

Width:
101'-4"

Depth:
110'-4"

Photo by Living Concepts

This home, as shown in the photograph, may differ from the actual blueprints.
For more detailed information, please check the floor plans carefully.

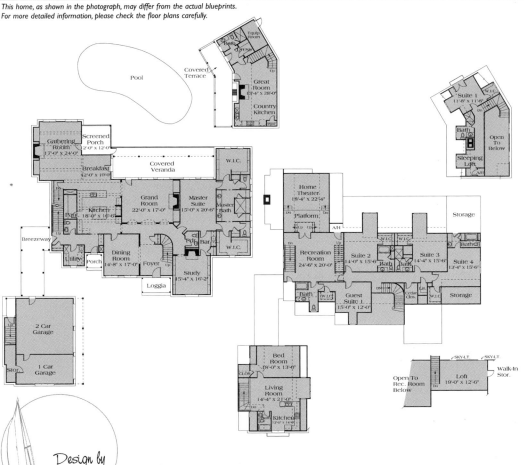

Design by
© **Living Concepts Home Planning**

Amenities abound in this opulent French country design, which includes a separate apartment or guest house and a two-story pool house. Entertaining is easy, with a central grand room and the formal dining room located right off the foyer. The heart of your gatherings, though, will be in the combination kitchen, breakfast nook and gathering room, where a fireplace and a private screened porch make this area warm and comfortable. Another favorite area will be the upper-level recreation room that opens, via French doors, to a home theater with a platform. While the sumptuous master suite is located on the first floor for privacy, four guest suites are available on the second floor. A skylit loft is tucked away on the third floor.

Design
A235

Basement:
1,688 sq. ft.

First Floor:
2,347 sq. ft.

Second Floor:
1,800 sq. ft.

Third Floor:
1,182 sq. ft.

Total:
7,017 sq. ft.

Width:
75'-5"

Depth:
76'-4"

This home, as shown in the photograph, may differ from the actual blueprints.
For more detailed information, please check the floor plans carefully.

If an opulent manor is cast for your future, this four-level plan has everything. Wake up in the master suite, step out on the lookout balcony to watch the sunrise over the lake, then take the elevator to the basement for a workout. Breakfast waits in the first-floor morning room, then a morning in the study takes care of the day's work, or go up to the second-floor reading nook. Three bedrooms on this floor share two baths and a veranda. Enjoy a relaxing hour in the master bath's garden tub, and select evening wear from a walk-in closet that doubles as a dressing room. After dinner in the formal dining room, view a new movie release in the home theater. The evening is complete with midnight supper in front of the fireplace in the gathering room—the end of a perfect day.

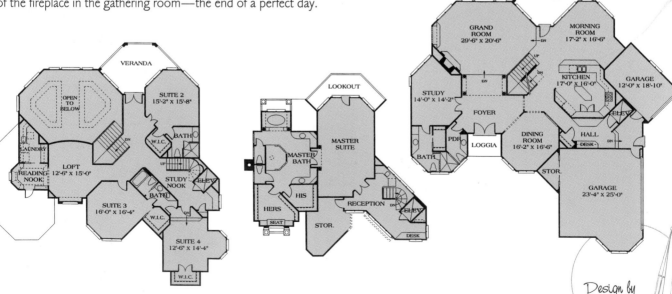

©Living Concepts Home Planning

Design
A302

First Floor:
2,538 sq. ft.

Second Floor:
1,581 sq. ft.

Total:
4,119 sq. ft.

Width:
67'-7"

Depth:
84'-5"

This home, as shown in the photographs, may differ from the actual blueprints. For more detailed information, please check the floor plans carefully.

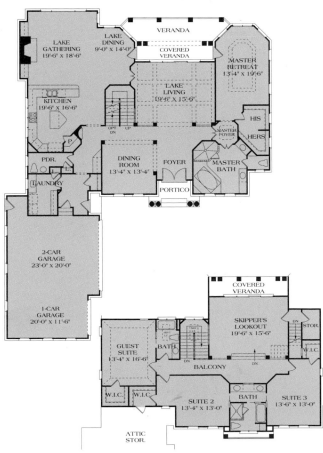

A double portico sets off this Southern-flavored facade, with double columns and a finely detailed balustrade. Inside, living areas are designed to take in views with walls of glass opening to a covered veranda. The lake gathering and dining area complements a formal dining room and a living room, which includes a spider-beam ceiling. The master suite has a luxury bath with a corner whirlpool tub and an oversized shower. The upper level includes a guest suite with its own walk-in closet.

Front View

Design by
©Living Concepts Home Planning

23

Design
A236

Basement:
1,707 sq. ft.

First Floor:
2,971 sq. ft.

Second Floor:
2,199 sq. ft.

Third Floor:
1,040 sq. ft.

Total:
7,917 sq. ft.

Width:
84'-4"

Depth:
69'-0"

Photos by Living Concepts

From the gathering room on the basement level to the master suite on the third floor, this plan provides a comfortable home, office, showplace, private retreat and entertainment center. The first floor includes living areas, a guest suite, a music room and an office. Three bedroom suites and a reception room are on the second floor. If four levels seems like a lot of space to cover, notice the elevator to the right of the front entrance. Altogether, this plan offers five bedrooms and five and a half bathrooms.

Rear View

This home, as shown in the photographs, may differ from the actual blueprints. For more detailed information, please check the floor plans carefully.

©Living Concepts Home Planning

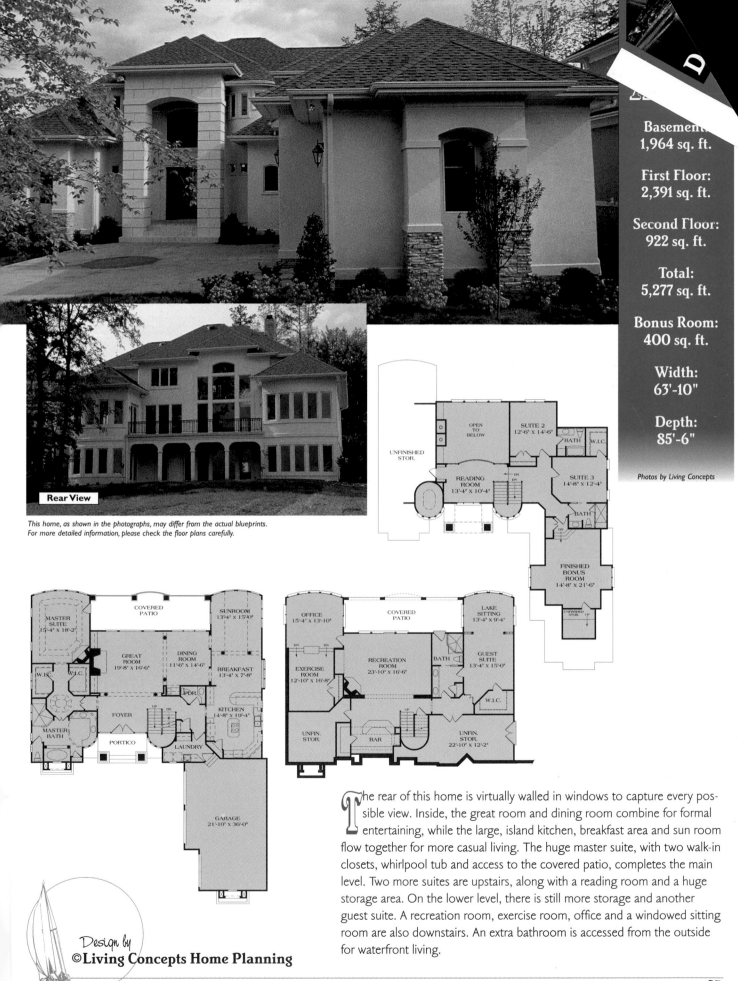

Basement:
1,964 sq. ft.

First Floor:
2,391 sq. ft.

Second Floor:
922 sq. ft.

Total:
5,277 sq. ft.

Bonus Room:
400 sq. ft.

Width:
63'-10"

Depth:
85'-6"

Photos by Living Concepts

Rear View

This home, as shown in the photographs, may differ from the actual blueprints.
For more detailed information, please check the floor plans carefully.

Second Floor

- OPEN TO BELOW
- UNFINISHED STOR.
- SUITE 2 — 12'-6" x 14'-6"
- BATH
- W.I.C.
- READING ROOM — 13'-4" x 10'-4"
- SUITE 3 — 14'-8" x 12'-4"
- BATH
- FINISHED BONUS ROOM — 14'-8" x 21'-6"
- UNFINISHED STOR.

First Floor

- MASTER SUITE — 15'-4" x 18'-2"
- COVERED PATIO
- SUNROOM — 13'-4" x 15'-0"
- W.I.C.
- W.I.C.
- GREAT ROOM — 19'-8" x 16'-6"
- DINING ROOM — 11'-6" x 14'-6"
- BREAKFAST — 13'-4" x 7'-8"
- PDR.
- MASTER BATH
- FOYER
- KITCHEN — 14'-8" x 19'-4"
- PORTICO
- LAUNDRY
- GARAGE — 21'-10" x 36'-0"

Basement

- OFFICE — 15'-4" x 13'-10"
- COVERED PATIO
- LAKE SITTING — 13'-4" x 9'-4"
- EXERCISE ROOM — 12'-10" x 16'-8"
- RECREATION ROOM — 23'-10" x 16'-6"
- BATH
- GUEST SUITE — 13'-4" x 15'-0"
- W.I.C.
- UNFIN. STOR.
- BAR
- UNFIN. STOR. — 22'-10" x 12'-2"

The rear of this home is virtually walled in windows to capture every possible view. Inside, the great room and dining room combine for formal entertaining, while the large, island kitchen, breakfast area and sun room flow together for more casual living. The huge master suite, with two walk-in closets, whirlpool tub and access to the covered patio, completes the main level. Two more suites are upstairs, along with a reading room and a huge storage area. On the lower level, there is still more storage and another guest suite. A recreation room, exercise room, office and a windowed sitting room are also downstairs. An extra bathroom is accessed from the outside for waterfront living.

Design by
© **Living Concepts Home Planning**

Design T017

First Floor:
1,900 sq. ft.

Second Floor:
800 sq. ft.

Total:
2,700 sq. ft.

Width:
63'-0"

Depth:
51'-0"

Photo by Dave Dawson

This home, as shown in the photograph, may differ from the actual blueprints. For more detailed information, please check the floor plans carefully.

A perfect blend of stucco and stacked stone sets off keystones, transoms and arches in this French country facade to inspire an elegant spirit. The foyer is flanked by the spacious dining room and the study, which is accented by a vaulted ceiling and a fireplace. A great room with a full wall of glass connects the interi-or with the outdoors. A first-floor master suite offers both style and intimacy with a coffered ceiling and a secluded bath. Upstairs, three family bedrooms share a hall bath. This home is designed with a basement foundation.

QUOTE ONE®
Cost to build? See page 198 to order complete cost estimate to build this house in your area!

Design by
Stephen Fuller

Design
T177

First Floor:
2,058 sq. ft.

Second Floor:
712 sq. ft.

Total:
2,770 sq. ft.

Width:
57'-3"

Depth:
81'-3"

If you've always dreamed of owning a villa, we invite you to experience this European lifestyle—on a perfectly manageable scale. This home offers the best of traditional formality and casual elegance. The foyer leads to the great room with a bold but stylish fireplace and three French doors to the rear terrace—sure to be left open during fair weather. The large kitchen opens gracefully to a private dining room that accesses a covered outdoor patio. The master suite combines great views with a sumptuous bath to complete this winning design. Upstairs, a balcony hall overlooking the great room leads to two family bedrooms that share a full hall bath. This home is designed with a basement foundation.

Design by
Stephen Fuller

Design
Y016

Main Level:
2,650 sq. ft.

Lower Level:
409 sq. ft.

Total:
3,059 sq. ft.

Width:
79'-0"

Depth:
77'-8"

This transitional home has space that can be converted either as the family grows or as it moves out and less space is needed. From its foyer, a study/bedroom opens to the left and features access to a bath. Another area worth noting is the basement. The rooms here can be used as either a garage/storage area and a bedroom, office or hobby room. Amenities abound in the master suite, which includes a uniquely shaped whirlpool tub in its lavish bathroom. The efficient kitchen offers easy access to both the formal dining room and more casual breakfast room. Note the hobby room off the garage.

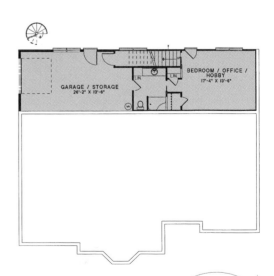

Design
Y046

First Floor:
1,400 sq. ft.

Second Floor:
743 sq. ft.

Total:
2,143 sq. ft.

Width:
58'-0"

Depth:
28'-0"

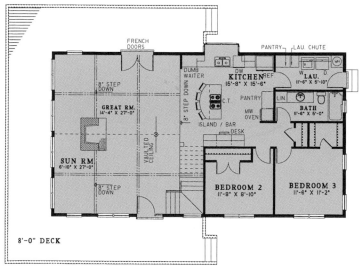

This attractive three-bedroom home would do well located at either the lakeshore or at the riverside. With soaring windows overlooking a wraparound deck off the spacious great room and sun room, entertaining will be a breeze. A fireplace adds warmth to the great room and can be viewed from the large kitchen. Here, a built-in desk, a cooktop island/snack bar and a dumb waiter will make the gourmet of the family truly happy. Two family bedrooms share a full bath and have easy access to the laundry room, completing this level. Upstairs, a lavish master suite awaits to pamper the homeowners. Its amenities cover all of the contingencies: a sink and a fridge—with a dumb waiter!; a full bath with a linen closet, separate tub and shower and a laundry chute; a fireplace; a vaulted ceiling with two sky lights; a private balcony-deck; two walk-in closets and separate office space

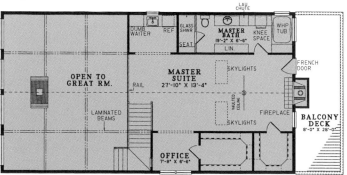

Design
T183

Square footage:
2,019

Bonus Loft:
363 sq. ft.

Width:
56'-0"

Depth:
56'-3"

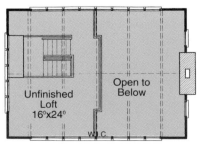

This design takes inspiration from the casual fishing cabins of the Pacific Northwest and interprets it for modern livability. It offers three options for a main entrance. One door opens to a mud porch, where a small hall leads to a galley kitchen and the vaulted great room. Two French doors on the side porch open into a dining room with bay-window seating. Another porch entrance opens directly into the great room. The great room is centered around a massive stone fireplace and is accented with a beautiful wall of windows. The secluded master bedroom features a master bath with a claw-foot tub and twin pedestal sinks, as well as a separate shower and walk-in closet. Two more bedrooms share a spacious bath. Ideal for a lounge or extra sleeping space, an unfinished loft looks over the great room.

Design by
Stephen Fuller

First Floor:
1,341 sq. ft.

Second Floor:
598 sq. ft.

Total:
1,939 sq. ft.

Width:
50'-3"

Depth:
46'-3"

© American Home Gallery, Ltd.

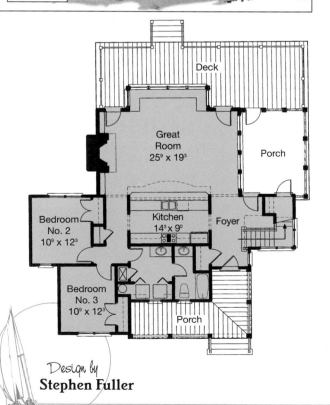

Front View

With horizontal siding, plentiful windows and a wraparound porch, this home is designed for comfort as well as presenting a pleasant facade. The great room is aptly named, with a fireplace, built-in seating and access to the rear deck. Meal preparation is a breeze with a galley kitchen designed for efficiency. A screened porch is available for sipping lemonade on warm summer afternoons. The first floor contains two bedrooms and a unique bath to serve family and guests. The second floor offers a private getaway with a master suite that supplies panoramic views from its adjoining sitting area. A master bath with His and Hers walk-in closets and a private deck complete the upstairs.

Deck

Great Room
25^9 x 19^3

Porch

Bedroom No. 2
10^9 x 12^3

Kitchen
14^3 x 9^0

Foyer

Bedroom No. 3
10^9 x 12^3

Porch

Open To Below

Deck

Sitting Area

Master Bedroom
14^3 x 14^3

Design by
Stephen Fuller

Design
T186

First Floor:
1,578 sq. ft.

Second Floor:
1,324 sq. ft.

Total:
2,902 sq. ft.

Bonus Room:
352 sq. ft.

Width:
76'-0"

Depth:
77'-9"

Shingles, shutters and vertical siding lend country cottage appeal to this home. The foyer leads to family living space, featuring a great room with a spider-beam ceiling, a bumped-out bay window and a focal-point fireplace. A guest bedroom enjoys a compartmented vanity and full bath. Upstairs, an L-shaped hall connects a master suite and two family bedrooms, which share a full bath with compartmented vanities. This home is designed with a basement foundation.

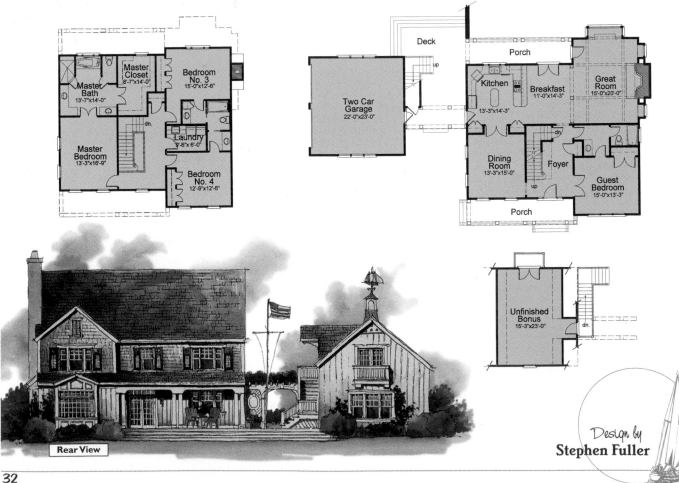

Rear View

Design by
Stephen Fuller

BY THE RIVER'S EDGE

Designs for riverside living

Design T183 by Stephen Fuller. See page 30 for details

"I've often wish'd

that I clear,

For life,

six hundred

pounds a year;

A handsome house

to lodge a friend,

A river at

my garden's end"

Alexander Pope

Design
2439

Square Footage: 1,312

Width: 40'-0"

Depth: 60'-0"

Here is a wonderfully organized plan with an exterior that will command the attention of each and every passerby. The rooflines and the pointed glass gable-end wall will be noticed immediately—the delightful deck will be quickly noticed, too, and is perfect for sunbathing or watching the water ripple by. Inside, visitors will be thrilled by the spaciousness of the huge living room. The ceilings slope upward to the exposed ridge beam. A free-standing fireplace will make its contribution to a cheerful atmosphere. The sleeping zone has two bedrooms, two bunk rooms, two full baths, two built-in chests and fine closet space.

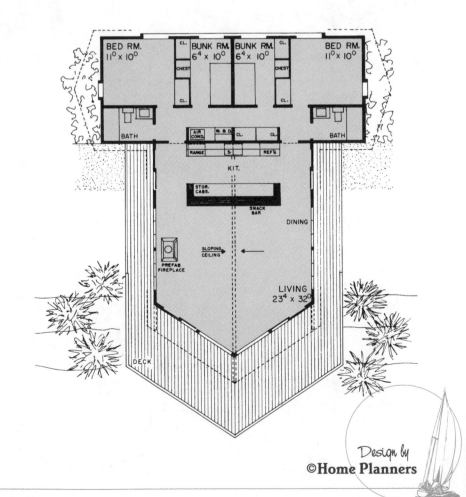

Design by
©Home Planners

Design Q429

Square Footage: 1,230

Width: 55'-6"

Depth: 30'-0"

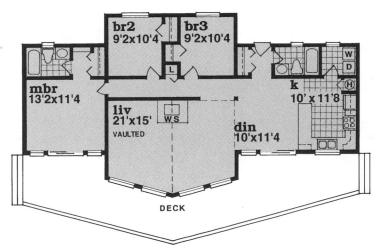

br2 9'2x10'4

br3 9'2x10'4

mbr 13'2x11'4

liv 21'x15' VAULTED

din 10'x11'4

k 10' x 11'8

W D

L

W.S

DECK

This is a grand vacation or retirement home, designed for views and the outdoor lifestyle. The full-width deck complements the abundant windows in rooms facing its way. The living room is made for gathering. It features a vaulted ceiling, a fireplace and full-height windows overlooking the deck. Open to this living space is the dining room with sliding glass doors to the outdoors and a pass-through counter to the U-shaped kitchen. The kitchen connects to a laundry area and has a window over the sink for more outdoor views. Two family bedrooms sit in the middle of the plan and share a full bath. The master suite has a private bath and deck views. The basement option for this plan adds 1,296 square feet to its total and extends the depth to 33 feet.

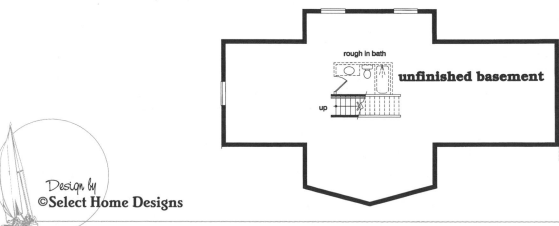

rough in bath

up

unfinished basement

Design by
©Select Home Designs

Design 3496

L

Square
Footage:
2,033

Width:
47'-6"

Depth:
61'-6"

COVERED PATIO

MASTER
BEDRM
12⁸ × 16⁴

SLOPED CEILING

WIC

M BATH

LIN

GARDEN
TUB

FAMILY
17⁸ × 14⁶

SLOPED CEILING

SNACK BAR

DINING
12⁰ × 15⁰

SLOPED CEILING

DESK

KITCHEN
17² × 12⁰

RANGE

REFG

SHELF

WETBAR

PANT

SLOPED CEILING

DN

RAILING

BATH

LIN

W D

RAISED HEARTH

LIVING
17⁶ × 14²

BEDRM
10² × 10⁶

BEDRM
11⁶ × 12⁰

SLOPED CEILING

COVERED PORCH

RAILING

Get more out of your homebuilding dollars with this unique one-story bungalow. A covered front porch provides sheltered entry into a spacious living room. A bookshelf and a column are special touches. The dining room enjoys a sloped ceiling, a wet bar and direct access to the rear covered patio. In the nearby kitchen, a breakfast bar accommodates quick meals. The adjacent family room rounds out this casual living area. The large master suite pampers with a sitting area, patio access and a luxurious bath that features a corner tub, a separate shower and dual lavatories. Two secondary bedrooms share a full hall bath.

QUOTE ONE®
Cost to build? See page 198
to order complete cost estimate
to build this house in your area!

Design by
©Home Planners

Square
Footage:
2,135

Width:
80'-8"

Depth:
60'-10"

You'll savor the timeless style of this charming bungalow design. With pleasing proportions, it welcomes all to its expansive front porch—perfect for quiet conversations. Inside, livability excels with a side-facing family kitchen. Here, an interesting bumped-out nook facilitates the placement of a built-in table and bench seats. A formal dining room rests to the rear of the plan and enjoys direct access to a back porch. The parlor, with a central fireplace, also accesses this outdoor living area. The master bedroom is just a step away from the living room. It offers large dimensions and a private bath with a walk-in closet, dual lavs and a bumped-out tub. An additional bedroom may also serve as a study.

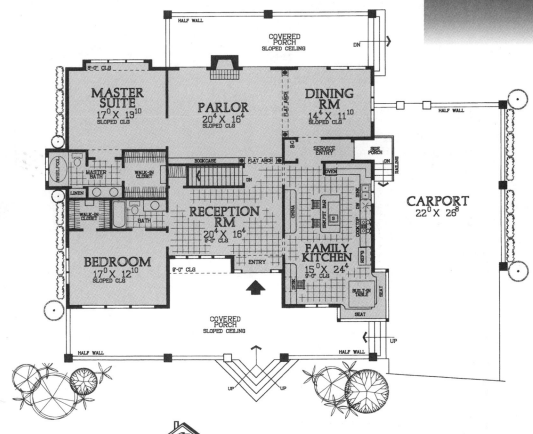

Design by
©Home Planners

Quote One®

Cost to build? See page 198
to order complete cost estimate
to build this house in your area!

Design Y047

Square Footage: 2,607

Width: 75'-4"

Depth: 81'-0"

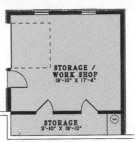

STORAGE / WORK SHOP
19'-10" X 17'-4"

STORAGE
3'-10" X 19'-10"

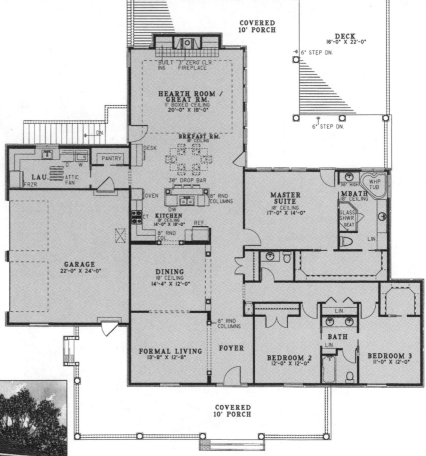

COVERED 10' PORCH

DECK
16'-0" X 22'-0"

6' STEP DN.

6' STEP DN.

BUILT 3" ZERO CLR. INS FIREPLACE

HEARTH ROOM / GREAT RM.
11' BOXED CEILING
20'-0" X 18'-0"

DESK

BREAKFAST RM.
8' CEILING

30" DROP BAR

MASTER SUITE
10' CEILING
17'-0" X 14'-0"

36" HIGH

WHP TUB

MBATH
10' CEILING

GLASS SHWR SEAT

LIN

PANTRY

LAU.
FRZR ATTIC FAN

OVEN

8' RND COLUMNS

DW

KITCHEN
8' CEILING
14'-0" X 18'-0"

REF

8' RND COL

GARAGE
22'-0" X 24'-0"

DINING
10' CEILING
14'-4" X 12'-0"

8' RND COLUMNS

LIN

BATH

LIN

FORMAL LIVING
13'-8" X 12'-8"

FOYER

BEDROOM 2
12'-0" X 12'-0"

BEDROOM 3
11'-0" X 12'-0"

COVERED 10' PORCH

This charming home has columned covered porches both front and back. To the left of the entry are the living and dining rooms, both defined by columns. The large open kitchen has a snack-bar and breakfast area, and flows into the great room, which has a fireplace as the focal point. The bedrooms are grouped to the right, including two family bedrooms sharing a compartmented bath, and the master suite with a whirlpool tub. The lower floor is one large storage area. Please specify slab or crawlspace foundation when ordering.

Rear View

Square Footage:
2,310

Width:
54'-6"

Depth:
97'-7"

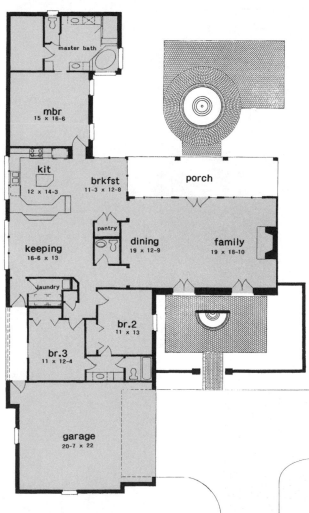

master bath

mbr
15 x 16-6

kit
12 x 14-3

brkfst
11-3 x 12-8

porch

pantry

keeping
16-6 x 13

dining
19 x 12-9

family
19 x 18-10

laundry

br.2
11 x 13

br.3
11 x 12-4

garage
20-7 x 22

This home boasts a beautiful entry courtyard that opens to the combined dining and family rooms through two sets of double doors. Here, a cheerful fireplace and a wall of windows with another French door add to the charm. Down the hall, past the convenient powder room, is a keeping room, an island kitchen—with a snack bar—and a breakfast area. Two family bedrooms at the front of the plan share a compartmented bath between them. The secluded master suite in the back includes a large closet and a corner tub surrounded by windows.

Design by
©Andy McDonald Design Group

Design M511

Square Footage: 2,678

Width: 69'-4"

Depth: 84'-8"

Old world charm is abundant in this French country home. The double-door entry is flanked by the living and dining rooms, and proceeds into the hearth-warmed family room. The large kitchen has a work island, a breakfast area and convenient access to the laundry room. The master bedroom, including a sitting area full of windows and a lavish bath with corner tub, is secluded at the rear of the plan. Three other bedrooms complete the plan, one of which has a private bath.

sitting
13 X 10-6

m bath

mbr
13-10 X 14-5

porch

br.2
11-2 X 12-10

family
19-2 X 19

brkfst
11-2 X 11

kit
13-6 X 15-11

br.3
11 X 11

living
(opt study)
16 X 10-10

foyer

dining
14-7 X 12

laundry

br.4
12-6 X 11-9

terrace

garage
22-7 X 21

Square
Footage:
2,364

Width:
62'-5"

Depth:
87'-4"

A wood-shingle roof caps this gra-cious stucco-and-brick home. The thoughtful design includes a back porch and a courtyard area visi-ble from many of the home's rooms. The foyer opens to the dining room to the left and the family room to the right. A walk-in pantry highlights the kitchen, which opens into the sunny breakfast area. Sleeping quarters include a master suite with a bayed sitting area and a huge walk-in closet, two family bedrooms with a shared bath and a separate fourth bedroom that could serve as a home office or guest quarters. This welcoming home is ideal for families large or small.

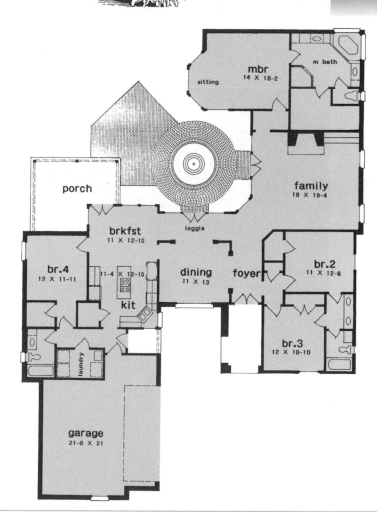

Design by
©Andy McDonald Design Group

Design M513

Square Footage:
2,625

Width:
67'-6"

Depth:
87'-1"

sitting
13 X 10-5

m bath

mbr
14-6 X 13-10

family
19 X 19

br.2
11 X 12-6

brkfst
16-4 X 12

to opt. bonus rm.

br.3
11 X 11

kit
16 X 14-6

laundry

dining
12 X 12

foyer

living
12 X 11

br.4
11 X 12

garage
22 X 20-6

Arch-top windows, transoms and shutters set off this beautiful European-style home. Formal rooms flank the foyer, which opens to a spacious family room with a fireplace and a wall of windows. The kitchen has a cooktop island and a bright breakfast area with a private porch. A stunning master suite features a sitting area, two large walk-in closets and a lavish bath with a garden tub and separate vanities. Two secondary bedrooms share a hall bath.

©Andy McDonald Design Group

Design by

Design
M526

Square Footage:
3,430

Width:
78'-9"

Depth:
79'-4"

sitting
7-2 x 9-5

master bath

mbr
17-1 x 18

solarium
20 x 9-6

brkfst
12-10 x 13-8

pantry

br.4
14-6 x 14-6

br.3
11-6 x 12-4

family
22 x 21

kit
13-6 x 15-4

laundry

butler

foyer

dining

storage
3-6 x 16-2

br.2
12-6 x 11-6

living rm
(opt. study)
11-8 x 14

garage
20-6 x 21

Rustic shutters and wood shingles give a definite Old World flavor to this home. Inside, though, there is every modern convenience. The large, open family room, breakfast area and well-appointed kitchen form the heart of this plan. A large, bright solarium at the rear makes a wonderful spot for relaxing or enjoying the view. The master bedroom has a sitting area with plenty of windows and a luxurious bath with corner tub. Three other bedrooms, one with a private bath, accommodate family or friends comfortably.

Design by
©Andy McDonald Design Group

Design M505

Square Footage:
2,322

Width:
68'-11"

Depth:
74'-0"

This European design combines brick and stucco, arched windows, a dormer above the French-door entry and a steeply pitched wood-shingle roof. The entry foyer opens directly to the family room with fireplace. A loggia to the left of the foyer provides a perfect place for floor-to-ceiling bookshelves, or would work as an art gallery. The well-designed kitchen, with its large pantry, opens to a breakfast area with porch access for dining alfresco. The garage entrance to the kitchen saves wear and tear on you and the house. Four bedrooms, including a sumptuous master suite, two full baths, a powder room and a generous laundry facility complete the home.

Design by

This comfortable European design marries a chateau spirit with a compact footprint. Open casual space and formal rooms invite gatherings planned and cozy. A wall of windows flows across the family and breakfast area, providing plenty of natural light. The breakfast area shares the warmth of the family room's fireplace and features access to a private porch. The homeowners' retreat offers its own fireplace, a spacious bath and a nearby study with its own bath. Two secondary bedrooms on the left side of the home share a bath, while a third bedroom on the far right side has access to a hall bath.

m bath

sitting

mbr
15 X 18

porch

brkfst
12-9 X 12

pantry

br.2
12-6 X 12

br.3
11-4 X 12-9

family
22 X 21

kit
15 X 16

laundry

br.4
11-6 X 12-6

living
11-8 X 14

foyer

dining
12 X 16

garage
20-2 x 24-2

Design by
©**Andy McDonald Design Group**

Design F131

Square Footage: 2,529

Width: 78'-2"

Depth: 50'-2"

This charming home grabs attention with a beautiful facade including corner quoins, symmetrical design and a lovely roofline. The floor plan holds great livability. A central great room connects to the breakfast room and galley-style kitchen. A formal dining room, just off the foyer, has a huge wall of windows for elegant dining. A complementary room to the left of the foyer serves as a den or guest bedroom as needed. The master bedroom features a tray ceiling and wonderfully appointed bath. A family bedroom to the front of the plan has a vaulted ceiling. Don't miss the screened porch to the rear of the plan.

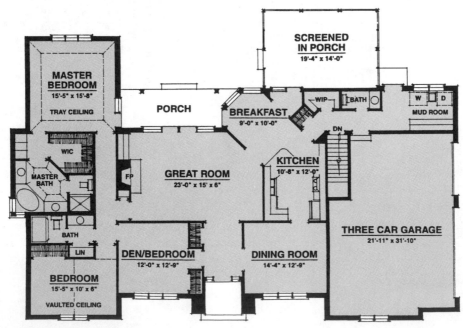

MASTER BEDROOM 15'-5" x 15'-8" TRAY CEILING

PORCH

SCREENED IN PORCH 19'-4" x 14'-0"

BREAKFAST 9'-0" x 10'-0"

WIP · BATH

W · D MUD ROOM

WIC

MASTER BATH

FP

GREAT ROOM 23'-0" x 15'-6"

KITCHEN 10'-8" x 12'-0"

DN

THREE CAR GARAGE 21'-11" x 31'-10"

BATH

LIN

DEN/BEDROOM 12'-0" x 12'-9"

DINING ROOM 14'-4" x 12'-9"

BEDROOM 15'-5" x 10'-6" VAULTED CEILING

Design by ©R.L. Pfotenhauer

Design
M512

Square
Footage:
2,706

Width:
73'-0"

Depth:
84'-11"

sitting
13 X 10-5

mbr
14-6 X 13-10

br.2
11 X 12-6

family
19 X 19

brkfst
16 X 12

br.3
11 X 11

foyer

study
12-4 X 10-11

dining
15-8 X 13-1

br.4
11-6 X 10-9

garage
20 X 20

Asymmetrical gables complement a stone-and-stucco facade on this lovely European-style design. Inside, formal rooms and casual space cluster around the open foyer and enjoy warmth from a fireplace and light from walls of windows, which offer views of the nearby riverfront. Two family bedrooms share a full bath, while a third bedroom—perfect for a guest suite—is located to the far left side of the home, away from traffic. The master suite has a tray ceiling, two walk-in closets and a compartmented bath.

Design by
© Andy McDonald Design Group

Design M517

First Floor:
2,298 sq. ft.

Second Floor:
731 sq. ft.

Total:
3,029 sq. ft.

Width:
71'-10"

Depth:
78'-0"

porch

brkfst
16 X 23-6

keeping

kit
12-9 X 15

family
20-2 X 19

dining
14 X 14

foyer

mbr
15 X 16-7

laundry

m bath

br. 2
11-10 X 11

garage
18-1 X 21

11-1 X 21

terrace

br. 3
12-2 X 14-11

br. 4
11-6 X 11

A large informal area includes the island kitchen, breakfast area, keeping room—with a fire-place—and family room. A formal dining room provides outside access to the front through one of three sets of French doors. The laundry room is next to the master bedroom. Upstairs, two additional bedrooms share a bath with separate dressing areas. The family cars can room together while the Ferrari enjoys a separate bay in the three-car garage. Beautiful exterior detailing in the dormer windows, wood-shingle roof and shutters sets this home apart.

Design by

©Andy McDonald Design Group

Design
8252

First Floor:
2,687 sq. ft.

Second Floor:
1,630 sq. ft.

Total:
4,317 sq. ft.

Bonus Room:
216 sq. ft.

Width:
87'-1"

Depth:
76'-7"

Dormer windows complement classic square columns on this country estate home, gently flavored with a Southern-style facade. A two-story foyer opens to traditional rooms. Two columns announce the living room, which has a warming hearth. The formal dining room opens to the back covered porch, decked out with decorative columns. The first-floor master suite enjoys His and Hers walk-in closets, an oversized shower, a whirlpool tub and a windowed water closet, plus its own door to the covered porch. A well-appointed kitchen features a corner walk-in pantry and opens to a double-bay family room and breakfast area. Upstairs, each of two family bedrooms has a private vanity. A gallery hall leads past a study/computer room—with two window seats—to a sizable recreation area that offers a tower-room bay.

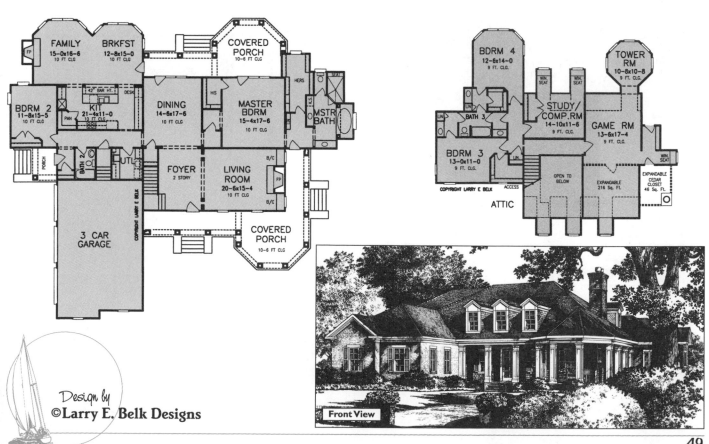

Front View

Design by
©Larry E. Belk Designs

Design M545

First Floor:
2,672 sq. ft.

Second Floor:
1,442 sq. ft.

Total:
4,114 sq. ft.

Width:
39'-4"

Depth:
97'-4"

Perfect for narrow river lots, this two-story home also offers plenty of windows to the rear to enjoy the view! The foyer is flanked by the master suite to the right and access to the garage and laundry to the left, with a staircase leading up to the second floor. Double doors are secreted under the staircase and lead to a spacious library. A dining room is next in line, defined by columns and across the hall from French doors to the outdoors. At the rear of the home, a spacious family room features a fireplace, built-in shelves and two sets of French doors. The U-shaped kitchen is complete with a cooktop island and an adjacent bayed breakfast area. Upstairs, three bedrooms and a large game room share two full baths.

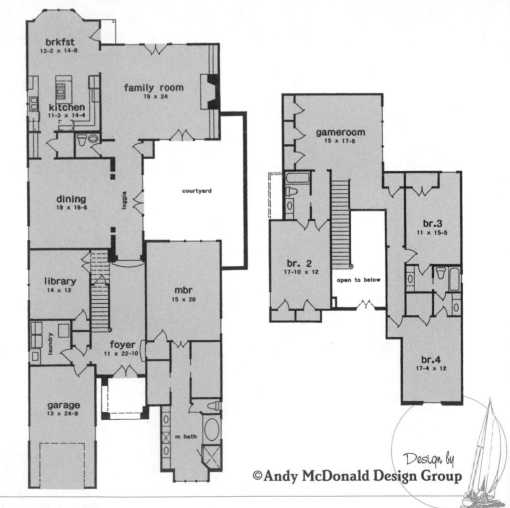

brkfst
13-2 x 14-8

family room
19 x 24

kitchen
11-3 x 14-4

dining
18 x 16-6

loggia

courtyard

library
14 x 12

mbr
15 x 20

laundry

foyer
11 x 22-10

garage
13 x 24-9

m bath

gameroom
15 x 17-8

br. 2
17-10 x 12

open to below

br.3
11 x 15-5

br.4
17-4 x 12

©Andy McDonald Design Group

Design by

Design M528

First Floor:
2,623 sq. ft.

Second Floor:
935 sq. ft.

Total:
3,558 sq. ft.

Width:
67'-6"

Depth:
79'-3"

The street view of this fine four-bedroom home is just the start of its charm—the rear offers an expanse of windows perfect for riverside views while amenities abound inside. The foyer is flanked by a formal living room (or make it a study) and a formal dining room. The family room features a warming fireplace, built-in bookshelves and a two-story wall of windows. The C-shaped kitchen is full of counter and cabinet space and includes a cooktop island and a large pantry. An adjacent breakfast room is surrounded by windows, offering early morning sunshine. The first-floor master suite is quite lavish and includes two walk-in closets, two vanities and a separate tub and shower. Finishing off this floor is a secluded bedroom and full bath, perfect for guests. Upstairs, two bedrooms share a bath and have access to a loft-like game room.

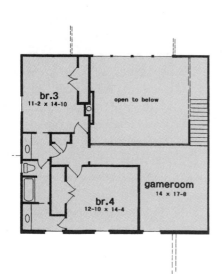

Design by
©Andy McDonald Design Group

Design M536

First Floor:
2,483 sq. ft.

Second Floor:
889 sq. ft.

Total:
3,372 sq. ft.

Width:
49'-10"

Depth:
120'-11"

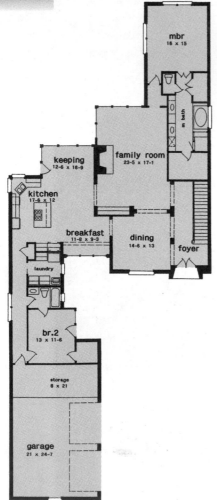

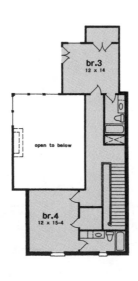

Designed for a narrow riverside lot, this two-story home is sure to please. The expanse of space occupied by the kitchen, keeping room and breakfast room is amazing and will bring a feeling of spaciousness to any gathering. The nearby formal dining room will easily accommodate your dinner parties, with after-dinner conversation nicely flowing into the adjacent family room to gather in front of the fireplace. Sleeping quarters on the first floor include the deluxe master suite and a secluded bedroom and full bath past the kitchen. The second floor is complete with two good-sized bedrooms—each with walk-in closets and private baths.

©Andy McDonald Design Group

Design by

Design E119

First Floor:
1,729 sq. ft.

Second Floor:
1,123 sq. ft.

Total:
2,852 sq. ft.

Bonus Room:
261 sq. ft.

Width:
60'-0"

Depth:
67'-6"

This nostalgic country design will bring a breath of fresh air to any neighborhood—in grand style. Past the wraparound porch, the open foyer expands to the stunning living area, with central fireplace and views from all three sides. Double French doors lead to the wraparound porch—to the right is a door leading back indoors through the cheery breakfast nook. Steps away, an angled breakfast bar also provides additional counter space for the kitchen, which is filled with convenient amenities. The master suite offers secluded luxury with a sizable walk-in closet, twin lavatories with vanity, and a windowed whirlpool tub. A convenient half bath at the service entrance curtails cross-traffic. Upstairs, a balcony hallway joins three family bedrooms and two full baths, and leads to a large, unfinished game room.

Storage
19'-8" X 7'-4"

Carport
20'-3" X 22'

Breakfast
12'-10" X 11'

Covered Porch

Util.

Ba.

Ma. Bath

Kitchen
12'-10" X 12'

Living
15'-3" X 25'

Master Bedroom
17'-8" X 13'

Foyer

Dining
12'-10" X 14'

Porch

Bedroom #2
12'-10" X 12'

Balcony

Bath

Unfinished Gameroom
17'-8" X 14'-8"

Bedroom #4
11'-6" X 14'

Bedroom #3
12'-10" X 13'

Bath

Design by
©Chatham Home Planning, Inc.

Design 8001

First Floor:
1,309 sq. ft.

Second Floor:
1,343 sq. ft.

Total:
2,652 sq. ft.

Width:
44'-4"

Depth:
58'-2"

Clean, contemporary lines set this home apart and make it a standout in any location. Inside, near the foyer, a 28-foot shaft opens from floor level to the top of the cupola. Remote control transoms in the cupola open automatically to increase ventilation. The great room, sun room, dining room and kitchen are all adjacent to provide areas for entertaining. Designed for a sloping riverside site, the home incorporates multiple levels inside. Additionally, there is access to a series of multi-level outside decks from the dining room, sun room and great room. All these areas have at least one glass wall overlooking the rear. The master bedroom and bath upstairs are bridged by a pipe rail balcony that provides access to a rear outside deck. The master suite includes a huge master closet. Additional storage and closet area is located off the hallway to the office.

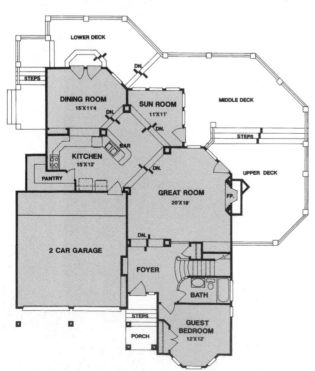

Design by
©Larry E. Belk Designs

Design
6690

First Floor:
876 sq. ft.

Second Floor:
948 sq. ft.

Total:
1,824 sq. ft.

Width:
27'-6"

Depth:
64'-0"

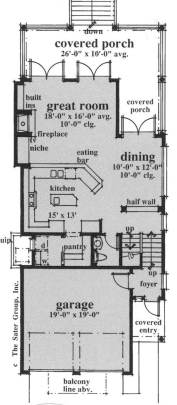

covered porch
26'-0" x 10'-0" avg.

down

built ins

great room
18'-0" x 16'-0" avg.
10'-0" clg.

covered porch

tv niche

fireplace

eating bar

dining
10'-0" x 12'-0"
10'-0" clg.

kitchen
15' x 13'

half wall

equip

d w pantry

up

up

foyer

garage
19'-0" x 19'-0"

covered entry

balcony line abv.

c The Sater Group, Inc.

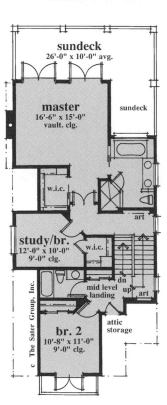

sundeck
26'-0" x 10'-0" avg.

master
16'-6" x 15'-0"
vault. clg.

sundeck

w.i.c.

art

study/br.
12'-0" x 10'-0"
9'-0" clg.

w.i.c.

dn up

art

mid level landing

br. 2
10'-8" x 11'-0"
9'-0" clg.

attic storage

c The Sater Group, Inc.

The captivating charm of this popular cottage calls up a sense of gentler times, with a quaint front balcony, horizontal siding and fishscale shingles. A contemporary, high-pitched roof harmonizes with sunbursts, double porticos and a glass-paneled entry. In the great room, lovely French doors bring the outside in, and a fireplace framed by built-in cabinetry adds warmth. The formal dining room opens to a private area of the covered porch. Double French doors with circle-head windows fill the master suite with sunlight and open to a private, sun-kissed deck.

Front View

Design 6701

First Floor:
876 sq. ft.

Second Floor:
1,245 sq. ft.

Total:
2,121 sq. ft.

Width:
27'-6"

Depth:
64'-0"

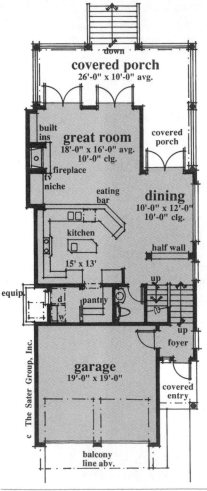

down

covered porch
26'-0" x 10'-0" avg.

built ins

great room
18'-0" x 16'-0" avg.
10'-0" clg.

fireplace

tv niche

covered porch

eating bar

dining
10'-0" x 12'-0"
10'-0" clg.

kitchen
15' x 13'

half wall

equip

d / w

pantry

up

up

foyer

garage
19'-0" x 19'-0"

covered entry

balcony line abv.

c The Sater Group, Inc.

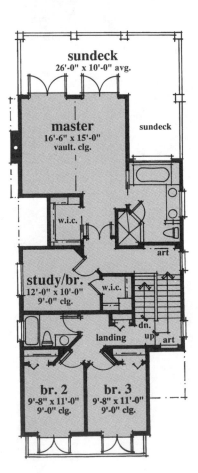

sundeck
26'-0" x 10'-0" avg.

master
16'-6" x 15'-0"
vault. clg.

sundeck

w.i.c.

art

study/br.
12'-0" x 10'-0"
9'-0" clg.

w.i.c.

landing

dn.

up

art

br. 2
9'-8" x 11'-0"
9'-0" clg.

br. 3
9'-8" x 11'-0"
9'-0" clg.

Key West Conch style blends Old World charm with New World comfort in this picturesque design. A glass-paneled entry lends a warm welcome and complements a captivating front balcony. The narrow floor plan works well—reminiscent of the Caribbean "shotgun" houses. Two sets of French doors open the great room to wide views and extend the living areas to the back covered porch. A gourmet kitchen is prepared for any occasion with a prep sink, plenty of counter space, an ample pantry and an eating bar. The mid-level landing leads to two additional bedrooms, a full bath and a windowed art niche. Double French doors open the upper-level master suite to a sun deck. Circle-head windows and a vaulted ceiling maintain a light and airy atmosphere. The master bath has a windowed soaking tub and a glass-enclosed walk-in shower. The plan offers the option of a fourth bedroom.

Design by

©The Sater Design Collection

Design 8002

First Floor:
1,530 sq. ft.

Second Floor:
968 sq. ft.

Total:
2,498 sq. ft.

Bonus Room:
326 sq. ft.

Width:
40'-0"

Depth:
66'-0"

The timeless influence of the French Quarter is exemplified in this home designed for river-front living. The double French-door entry opens into a large living room/dining room area separated by a double archway. A railed balcony with a loft on the second floor overlooks the living room. A pass-through between the kitchen and dining room also provides seating at a bar for informal dining. The spacious master bedroom at the rear includes a sitting area and a roomy master bath with a large walk-in closet. Two additional bedrooms, a bath and a bonus area for an office or game room are located upstairs.

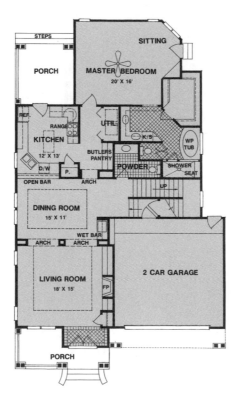

Design by
©**Larry E. Belk Designs**

Design 8052

First Floor:
904 sq. ft.

Second Floor:
1,058 sq. ft.

Total:
1,962 sq. ft.

Width:
22'-0"

Depth:
74'-0"

This fine clapboard home is reminiscent of the popular "shotgun" homes of the past. Designed for a narrow lot and perfect for urban or river-front living, this home features two balconies on the upper level. A two-way fireplace located between the formal living room and dining room provides visual impact. Built-in bookcases flanking arched openings between these rooms add drama. The sunny breakfast area and the efficient kitchen, with its convenient features, will be treasures valued by the busy cook. A pass-through from the kitchen to the dining room simplifies serving and a walk-in pantry provides lots of storage. On the second floor, the master bedroom provides access to a large balcony and the relaxing master bath is designed with a large separate shower and an angled whirlpool tub. Two secondary bedrooms and a full bath are located at the rear of the plan. This plan is available with either a crawlspace or slab foundation. Please specify when ordering.

GARAGE

COPYRIGHT 1993 LARRY E. BELK

BRKFST
10-6 X 11-4
10 FT CEILING

PAN

KITCHEN
11-6 X 10-6
10 FT CEILING

PATIO

FASS THRU

DINING ROOM
15-6 X 13-0
TRAYED CEILING

PWDR

TWO WAY
FP

ARCH   ARCH

LIVING ROOM
15-6 X 15-0
10 FT CEILING

ENTRY

PORCH

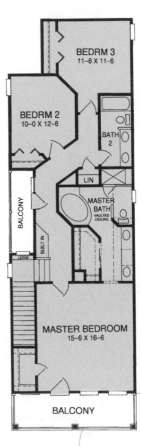

BEDRM 3
11-6 X 11-6

BEDRM 2
10-0 X 12-6

BATH 2

BALCONY

LIN

MASTER
BATH
VAULTED
CEILING

BUILT IN

LEDGE

MASTER BEDROOM
15-6 X 16-6

BALCONY

Design by

©**Larry E. Belk Designs**

Design 9534

First Floor:
762 sq. ft.

Second Floor:
738 sq. ft.

Total:
1,500 sq. ft.

Width:
34'-0"

Depth:
36'-0"

A s a starter or fine family home, this two-story design functions well. An attractive traditional exterior introduces the interior by way of a covered front porch. The living room opens directly off the foyer and features a fireplace and an expansive window seat. Sharing space with this area is the gourmet kitchen. It delights with an island cooktop, a sunny sink and a pantry. Room for a dinette set is right near a side door. Accommodations for a washer and dryer, a rear deck and a powder room complete the first floor. Upstairs, three bedrooms all include vaulted ceilings. The master bedroom enjoys its own private bath and a deck.

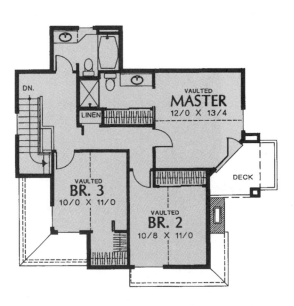

Design by
©Alan Mascord Design Associates, Inc.

Design Z233

First Floor:
858 sq. ft.

Second Floor:
502 sq. ft.

Total:
1,360 sq. ft.

Width:
35'-0"

Depth:
29'-8"

This fine brick home features a bay-windowed sun room, perfect for admiring the view. Inside this open floor plan, a family room features a fireplace and a spacious eat-in kitchen with access to the sun room. There are also a bedroom, full bath and laundry facilities on this floor. Upstairs there are two more bedrooms sharing a compartmented bath, as well as an overlook to the family room below. This home is designed with a basement foundation.

6,00 X 4,20
20'-0" X 14'-0"

3,60 X 3,60
12'-0" X 12'-0"

4,20 X 3,90

3,90 X 2,70
13'-0" X 9'-0"

3,00 X 3,30
10'-0" X 11'-0"

4,50 X 3,30
15'-0" X 11'-0"

Design 7631

First Floor:
1,750 sq. ft.

Second Floor:
604 sq. ft.

Total:
2,354 sq. ft.

Width:
64'-0"

Depth:
42'-8"

Rustic design invades contemporary detailing. The result? This fine two-story home. The front porch is expected and appreciated as a cozy outdoor retreat. Its mate is found at the back in another porch. The foyer leads to an immense great room with fireplace and cathedral ceiling, and to its attached formal dining space. This area opens to the U-shaped kitchen and cornered breakfast area.

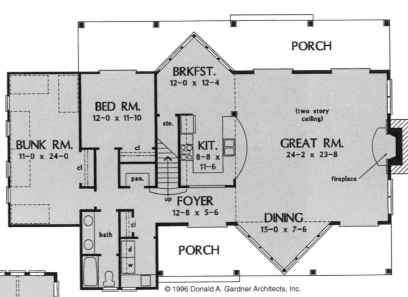

PORCH

BRKFST.
12-0 x 12-4

BED RM.
12-0 x 11-10

(two story ceiling)

BUNK RM.
11-0 x 24-0

KIT.
8-8 x 11-6

GREAT RM.
24-2 x 23-8

fireplace

sto.

cl

cl

pan.

up FOYER
12-8 x 5-6

DINING
15-0 x 7-6

bath

d
w

cl

PORCH

MASTER BED RM.
12-0 x 13-3

down

LOFT/ STUDY
8-5 x 16-10

great room below

master bath

lin.

exposed trusses

walk-in closet

A private bedroom and a bunk room are found to the left of the first floor. They share the use of a full bath. You might also turn the bunk room into two separate bedrooms; the choice is yours. The master suite holds forth on the second level. It has an attached study loft that overlooks the great room.

Design by
Donald A. Gardner Architects, Inc.

Design 4027

Square Footage: 1,320

Optional Finished Basement: 1,320 sq. ft.

Width: 52'-0"

Depth: 36'-0"

Good things come in small packages! The size and shape of this design will help hold down construction costs without sacrificing livability. The enormous great room is a multi-purpose living space with room for a dining area and several seating areas. Also notice the sloped ceilings. Sliding glass doors provide access to the wraparound deck and sweeping views of the outdoors.

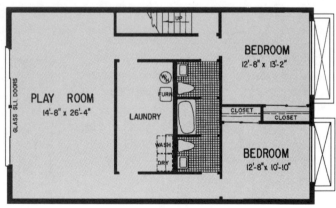

PLAY ROOM 14'-8" x 26'-4"

LAUNDRY

BEDROOM 12'-8" x 13'-2"

BEDROOM 12'-8" x 10'-10"

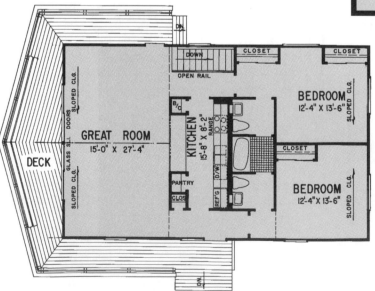

DECK

GREAT ROOM 15'-0" x 27'-4"

KITCHEN 15'-8" x 8'-2"

BEDROOM 12'-4" x 13'-6"

BEDROOM 12'-4" x 13'-6"

PANTRY

The well-equipped kitchen includes a pass-through and pantry. Two bedrooms on the main level, each with sloped ceilings and compartmented bath, round out the plan. The optional basement can be finished with two bedrooms, a laundry and a spacious play room.

Quote One

Cost to build? See page 198 to order complete cost estimate to build this house in your area!

Design by ©Home Planners

Design Q430

First Floor:
1,061 sq. ft.

Second Floor:
482 sq. ft.

Total:
1,543 sq. ft.

Width:
28'-0"

Depth:
39'-9"

A sun deck makes this design popular, but it is enhanced by views through an expansive wall of glass in the living and dining rooms. These rooms are warmed by a wood stove and enjoy vaulted ceilings, as well. The kitchen is also vaulted and has a prep island and breakfast bar. Behind the kitchen is a laundry room with side access. Two bedrooms and a full bath are found on the first floor. A skylit staircase leads up to the master bedroom and its walk-in closet and private bath on the second floor.

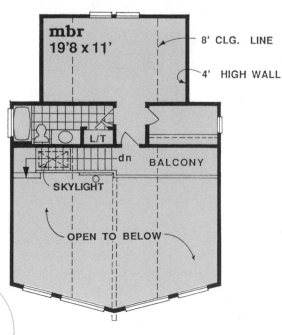

mbr
19'8 x 11'

8' CLG. LINE

4' HIGH WALL

L/T

dn BALCONY

SKYLIGHT

OPEN TO BELOW

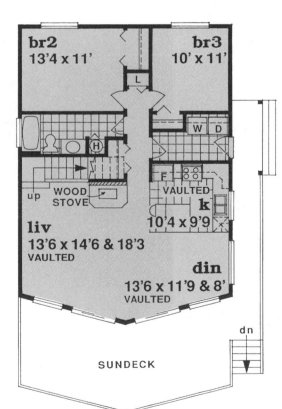

br2
13'4 x 11'

br3
10' x 11'

L

W D

up

WOOD STOVE

F

VAULTED

k
10'4 x 9'9

liv
13'6 x 14'6 & 18'3
VAULTED

din
13'6 x 11'9 & 8'
VAULTED

dn

SUNDECK

Design by
© Select Home Designs

63

Design Q519

First Floor:
1,375 sq. ft.

Second Floor:
284 sq. ft.

Total:
1,659 sq. ft.

Width:
58'-0"

Depth:
32'-0"

An expansive window wall across the great room of this home adds a spectacular view and accentuates the high ceiling. A corner wood stove warms the room in winter months. The open kitchen shares an eating bar with the dining room and features a convenient U shape.

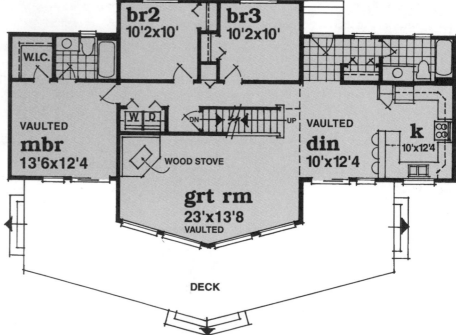

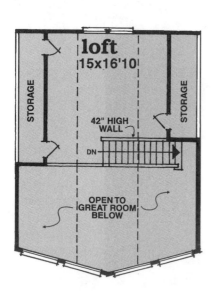

Sliding glass doors in the dining room lead to the deck. Two bedrooms sit to the back and share the use of a full bath. The loft on the upper level adds living or sleeping space and offers a wealth of storage space as well. Plans include both a basement and a crawlspace foundation.

Design by
©Select Home Designs

Design 9630

First Floor: 1,374 sq. ft.

Second Floor: 608 sq. ft.

Total: 1,982 sq. ft.

Width: 40'-0"

Depth: 60'-8"

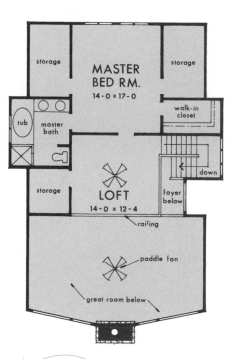

Second floor plan:
- storage
- MASTER BED RM. 14-0 × 17-0
- storage
- tub
- master bath
- walk-in closet
- storage
- LOFT 14-0 × 12-4
- down
- foyer below
- railing
- paddle fan
- great room below

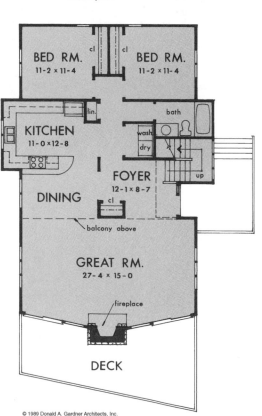

First floor plan:
- BED RM. 11-2 × 11-4
- cl
- cl
- BED RM. 11-2 × 11-4
- KITCHEN 11-0 × 12-8
- lin.
- bath
- wash
- dry
- up
- FOYER 12-1 × 8-7
- DINING
- cl
- balcony above
- GREAT RM. 27-4 × 15-0
- fireplace
- DECK

This rustic three-bedroom vacation home allows for casual living both inside and out. The two-story great room offers dramatic space for entertaining with windows stretching clear to the roof, maximizing the outdoor view. A rock fireplace is the focal point of this room. Two family bedrooms on the first floor share a full bath. The second floor holds the master bedroom with spacious master bath and walk-in closet. A large loft area overlooks the great room and entrance foyer.

Design by
Donald A. Gardner Architects, Inc.

Design 3697

First Floor:
586 sq. ft.

Second Floor:
486 sq. ft.

Total:
1,072 sq. ft.

Width:
40'-0"

Depth:
40'-0"

Surrounded by a covered porch for outdoor living, this cozy farmhouse could be a vacation getaway. The great room opens from the porch and features a fireplace and a nearby powder room. The L-shaped kitchen and dining nook access the rear porch, and there's space for a washer and dryer. Two upstairs bedroom suites have arched windows and private baths.

Quote One®
Cost to build? See page 198
to order complete cost estimate
to build this house in your area!

Design by
©**Home Planners**

Design 3683
LD

First Floor:
1,139 sq. ft.

Second Floor:
576 sq. ft.

Total:
1,715 sq. ft.

Width:
52'-0"

Depth:
46'-0"

A be Lincoln most likely would have looked upon this log home as a palace. And he would have been correct! A rustically royal welcome extends from the wraparound porch, inviting one and all into a comfortable interior. To the right of the foyer, a two-story great room, enhanced by a raised hearth fireplace, sets a spirited country mood. Nearby, a snack bar joins the living area with an efficient, U-shaped kitchen and an attached nook. Two family bedrooms, a full bath and a utility room with space for a washer and dryer complete the first floor. The second-floor master suite features amenities that create a private, restful getaway. Curl up in the window seat with a good book or enjoy fresh air from your own private balcony.

QUOTE ONE®

Cost to build? See page 198 to order complete cost estimate to build this house in your area!

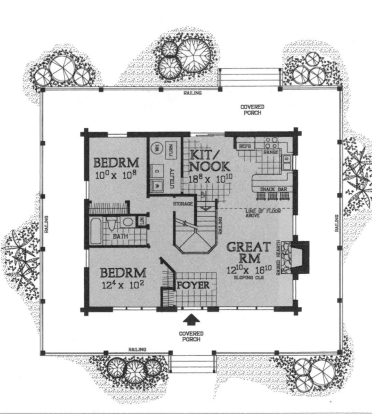

Design by
©Home Planners

Design 3682
LD

First Floor:
1,093 sq. ft.

Second Floor:
603 sq. ft.

Total:
1,696 sq. ft.

Width:
46'-0"

Depth:
52'-0"

This two-story home's rustic design reflects thoughtful planning, including a porch that fully wraps the house in comfort and provides lots of room for rocking. A stone chimney and arched windows set in dormers further enhance this home's country appeal. Inside, the floor plan is designed for maximum efficiency. A great room with a sloped ceiling enjoys a raised-hearth fireplace whose warmth radiates into the kitchen/nook. The master bedroom is located on the first floor and includes plenty of closet space and a master bath filled with amenities. A utility room and a powder room complete this level. The second floor contains two secondary bedrooms, a full bath and a loft/study with a window seat.

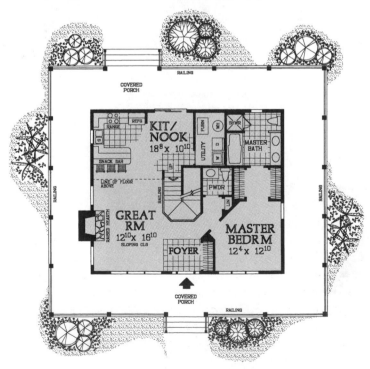

QUOTE ONE®
Cost to build? See page 198 to order complete cost estimate to build this house in your area!

Design by
©**Home Planners**

68

First Floor:
1,374 sq. ft.

Second Floor:
600 sq. ft.

Total:
1,974 sq. ft.

Width:
51'-8"

Depth:
50'-8"

NOOK
16⁰ x 10⁰

SNACK BAR

KIT
16⁰ x 10⁴

COVERED PORCH

LINE OF FLOOR ABOVE

GREAT RM
17¹⁰ x 21⁰
VOL CLG

POWDER RM

MASTER BATH

WHIRL-POOL

SHWR   LIN

FOYER
VOL CLG

WALK-IN CLOSET

UP

MASTER BEDRM
16⁰ x 13⁸

COVERED PORCH

RAILING

BEDRM
16⁰ x 10⁰

WALK-IN CLOSET

LINEN

DN

SEAT

BATH

OPEN TO BELOW

WALK-IN CLOSET

BEDRM
16⁰ x 10⁰

RAILING

QUOTE ONE®
Cost to build? See page 198
to order complete cost estimate
to build this house in your area!

Balustrades and brackets, dual balconies and a wraparound porch create a country-style exterior reminiscent of soft summer evenings spent watching fireflies and sipping sun tea. Indeed, an aura of hospitality prevails throughout the well-planned interior, starting with a tiled foyer that opens to an expansive two-story great room filled with light from six windows, a fireplace with tiled hearth and a sloped ceiling. A sunny, bayed nook invites casual dining and shares its natural light with a snack counter and a well-appointed U-shaped kitchen. A spacious master suite occupies the bay on the opposite side of the plan and offers a sumptuous bath with corner whirlpool tub, dual lavatories and a walk-in closet. Upstairs, two family bedrooms, each with a private balcony and a walk-in closet, share a full bath with twin lavs.

Design by
©Home Planners

Design N147

Main Level:
790 sq. ft.

Upper Level:
453 sq. ft.

Lower Level:
340 sq. ft.

Total:
1,583 sq. ft.

Width:
26'-4"

Depth:
30'-0"

Featuring a shed-style roofline and wraparound decks, this three-bedroom design is ideal for waterfront or wooded property. The decks provide sunny areas up top and shaded areas below. Skylights, fireplace and ample living space make the inside cozy and bright. A large living room with an adjacent kitchen sweeps into the enormous dining room with two skylights and a heat-circulating fireplace. The master bedroom has a private deck on the upper level. The lower level includes a third bedroom, a full bath and a laundry/utility room.

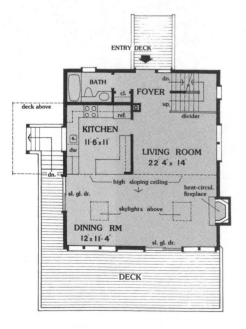

ENTRY DECK

BATH cl. FOYER dn.
KITCHEN 11'6 x 11' up. divider ref.
LIVING ROOM 22'4 x 14'
high sloping ceiling heat-circul. fireplace
skylights above
DINING RM 12' x 11'-4" sl. gl. dr.
deck above
dn.
DECK

BATH HALL dn.
lin.
MASTER BED RM 14 x 11 cl. BED RM 10'-9" x 9'-10"
DECK
sl. gl. dr. cl.
high windows above
skylight skylight
ROOF
deck below

ENTRY DECK ABOVE

BATH HALL cl. up.
lin. cl.
d. w. UTILITY
LAUNDRY 10'-10" x 10' cl. BED RM 12'-6" x 9'-8"
up.
DECK ABOVE

Design by
©**Perfect Home Plans, Inc.**

Design 3499
LD

First Floor:
1,836 sq. ft.

Second Floor:
600 sq. ft.

Total:
2,436 sq. ft.

Width:
86'-7"

Depth:
54'-0"

Rustic rafter tails and double columns highlight the front covered porch of this slightly rugged exterior, but sophisticated amenities abound inside and out—starting with the unique porte cochere and quiet side entrance to the home. To the left of the foyer, a formal dining room is bathed in natural light from two sets of triple windows. This area is easily served by a well-appointed kitchen with a built-in desk and a snack bar. A secluded master suite is replete with popular amenities: a garden tub with separate shower, knee-space vanity, dual lavatories and an adjoining study or sitting room. Upstairs, a balcony hall connects two additional bedrooms and a full bath—there's even space for a library or study area!

PORTE COCHERE

QUOTE ONE®

Cost to build? See page 198
to order complete cost estimate
to build this house in your area!

Design by
©**Home Planners**

Design 1404

Square Footage: 1,336

Width: 69'-2"

Depth: 39'-11"

H ere is an exciting design, unusual in character, yet fun to live in. This design, with its frame exterior and large glass areas, has as its dramatic focal point a hexagonal living area that gives way to interesting angles. The spacious living area features sliding glass doors through which traffic may pass to the terrace stretching across the entire length of the house. The wide overhanging roofs project over the terraces, thus providing partial protection from the weather. The sloping ceilings converge above the unique, open fireplace. The sleeping areas are located in each wing from the hexagonal center.

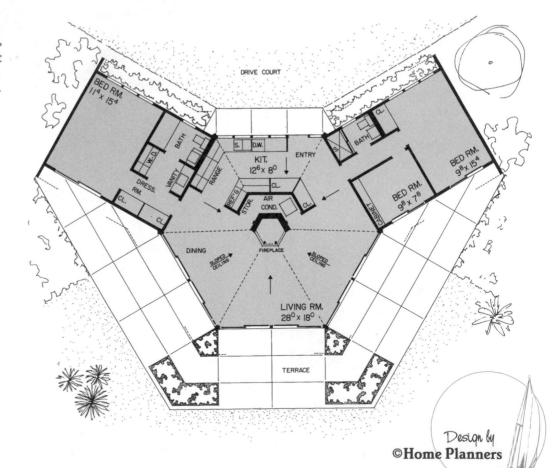

Design by
©Home Planners

Design
Q516

Square
Footage:
1,405

Width:
62'-0"

Depth:
29'-0"

This three-bedroom leisure home is perfect for the family that spends casual time out of doors. An expansive wall of glass gives a spectacular view to the great room and accentuates the high vaulted ceilings throughout the design. The great room is also warmed by a hearth and is open to the dining room and L-shaped kitchen. A triangular snack bar graces the kitchen and provides space for casual meals. Bedrooms are split, with the master bedroom on the right side of the plan and the family bedrooms on the left. The master suite has exposed beams in the ceiling, a walk-in closet and a full bath with soaking tub. Family bedrooms share a full bath. Plans include details for both a basement and a crawl-space foundation.

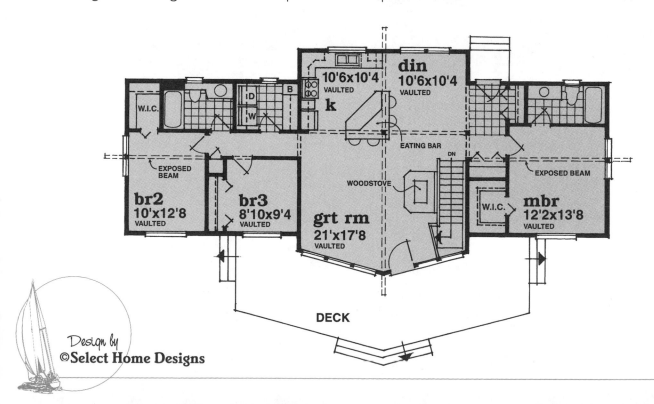

Design by
©Select Home Designs

Design N105

First Floor:
1,345 sq. ft.

Second Floor:
656 sq. ft.

Total:
2,001 sq. ft.

Width:
49'-0"

Depth:
58'-0"

Creative design at its best is evident in this two-story contemporary. A dramatic trellis-covered walkway leads into a vestibule with closet and on to the main living space. The combined living and dining room has a sixteen-foot ceiling, and a field-stone, heat-circulating fireplace flanked by unique scalloped windows. A semi-circle of windows forms the dinette space, creating a flood of light into the adjoining well-equipped kitchen. Two large bedrooms and a full bath with dual vanities and oversized whirlpool tub share the first-floor sleeping wing. Two additional bedrooms are upstairs, plus an optional den open to the living room below. Stairs off the center hall lead to the optional full basement. Please specify basement or slab foundation when ordering.

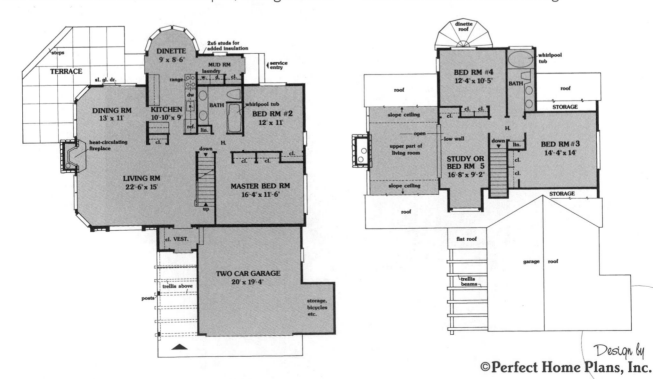

© Perfect Home Plans, Inc.

SEASHORE SILHOUETTES

Homes for living near the ocean

Design T175 by Stephen Fuller. See page 31 for details

"My life

is like a stroll

upon the beach—

As near

the ocean's edge

as I can go."

Henry David Thoreau

Design 6680

First Floor:
1,007 sq. ft.

Second Floor:
869 sq. ft.

Total:
1,876 sq. ft.

Width:
43'-8"

Depth:
53'-6"

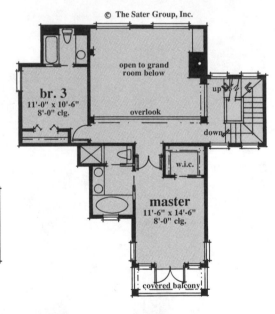

© The Sater Group, Inc.

open to grand room below

overlook

up

br. 3
11'-0" x 10'-6"
8'-0" clg.

down

w.i.c.

stair tower

down

master
11'-6" x 14'-6"
8'-0" clg.

covered balcony

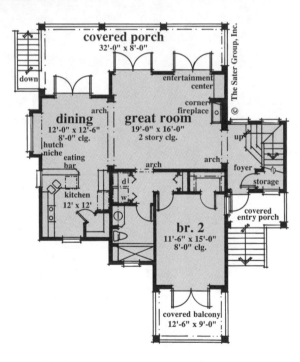

© The Sater Group, Inc.

covered porch
32'-0" x 8'-0"

down

entertainment center

corner fireplace

dining
12'-0" x 12'-6"
8'-0" clg.

arch

great room
19'-0" x 16'-0"
2 story clg.

hutch niche

eating bar

kitchen
12' x 12'

arch

arch

d
w

up

foyer

storage

covered entry porch

br. 2
11'-6" x 15'-0"
8'-0" clg.

covered balcony
12'-6" x 9'-0"

Front View

An enchanting center gable announces a graceful, honest architecture that's at home with the easygoing nature of this coastal design. Gentle arches add pleasing definition to an open interior. The well-appointed kitchen features a corner walk-in pantry, an eating bar for easy meals and an angled double sink. A gallery hall with a balcony overlook to the great room leads to an additional suite. Please specify basement or crawlspace foundation when ordering.

Design by
©**The Sater Design Collection**

First Floor:
1,290 sq. ft.

Second Floor:
548 sq. ft.

Total:
1,838 sq. ft.

Width:
38'-0"

Depth:
51'-0"

Front View

This eye-catching exterior features plenty of attractive windows, front and back porches and a variety of rooflines. The two-story great room is the heart of this home, with its corner fireplace, built-in entertainment center and eating bar. Arches lead into this room from the foyer, the spacious island kitchen and the formal dining room. A covered porch is accessible from the two main rooms as well as the master suite, which includes a deluxe private bath. On the second floor, Bedroom 2 offers access to a private deck. A third bedroom and full bath complete this floor. Please specify basement or crawlspace foundation when ordering.

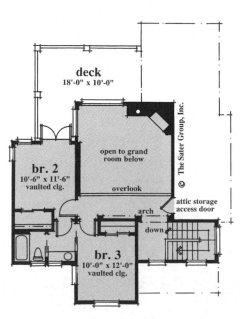

down

covered porch
18'-0" x 10'-0"

master
13'-0" x 15'-0"
vaulted clg.

© The Sater Group, Inc.

corner
fireplace

entertainment
center

w.i.c.

great room
16'-0" x 18'-0"
2 story clg.

dining
11'-0" x 13'-0"
8'-0" clg.

arch

arch

arch

eating
bar

arch

butlers
pantry

w/d

kitchen

storage

foyer

up

deck
18'-0" x 10'-0"

© The Sater Group, Inc.

open to grand
room below

br. 2
10'-6" x 11'-6"
vaulted clg.

overlook

arch

attic storage
access door

down

br. 3
10'-0" x 12'-0"
vaulted clg.

10' x 16'

covered entry porch

Design by
©**The Sater Design Collection**

First Floor:
1,383 sq. ft.

Second Floor:
595 sq. ft.

Total:
1,978 sq. ft.

Width:
48'-0"

Depth:
42'-0"

2 car garage

bonus/ storage

storage

deck

porch

porch

br. 3
11'-6" x 12'-0"
10'-0"h. clg.

br. 2
12'-10" x 12'-0"
10'-0"h. clg.

fireplace

built ins

great room
15'-0" x 19'-6"
vaulted clg.

covered porch

dining
11'-0" x 12'-8"
11'-0" tray clg.

kitchen
11'-0" x 12'-0"

up

up
foyer

stor.

util.

entry

porch

master suite
12'-8" x 17'-8"
10'-0" tray clg.

open to below

w.i.c.

master bath

overlook

dn

dn

porch

This fabulous Key West home blends interior space with the great outdoors. Designed for a balmy climate, this home boasts expansive porches and decks—with outside access from every area of the home. A sun-dappled foyer leads via a stately mid-level staircase to a splendid great room, which features a warming fireplace tucked in beside beautiful built-in cabinetry. Highlighted by a wall of glass that opens to the rear porch, this two-story living space serves as the stunning heart of the home, and opens to the formal dining room and the kitchen. Upstairs, a ten-foot tray ceiling highlights a very private master suite, which provides French doors to an upper-level porch. French doors open to decks and covered porches from a savory interior, and a high gallery overlooks the great room.

Design by
©The Sater Design Collection

First Floor:
954 sq. ft.

Second Floor:
348 sq. ft.

Lower Floor:
409 sq. ft.

Total:
1,711 sq. ft.

Width:
30'-0"

Depth:
40'-0"

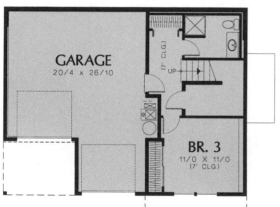

GARAGE
20/4 x 26/10

(7' CLG.)

UP

BR. 3
11/0 X 11/0
(7' CLG.)

Just right for a sloping lot on the beachfront, this home has a double garage at the lower level, along with a bedroom and a full bath. The main level contains living and dining space, graced by ten-foot ceilings. The L-shaped kitchen is defined and separated from the living areas by its island work space. A second bedroom and full bath are on the right side of the main level. The second floor contains a private, vaulted bedroom with a long wall closet and a compartmented bath with dual sinks. Note the open deck space just off the living room and facing to the front.

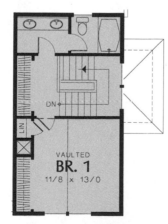

DN

LIN

VAULTED
BR. 1
11/8 x 13/0

BUILT-IN   BUILT-IN

W D

LIVING
13/0 x 17/0
(10' CLG.)

REF

UP   DN

DN

PAN

DINING
10/0 x 15/0
(10' CLG.)

BR. 2
14/0 x 10/0
(8' CLG.)

Design by
©**Alan Mascord Design Associates, Inc.**

Design 7515

First Floor:
898 sq. ft.

Second Floor:
777 sq. ft.

Total:
1,675 sq. ft.

Width:
34'-0"

Depth:
38'-0"

Shingle siding covers this narrow home, creating an exterior that weathers and improves with age. The open interior begins with the main level, where the living room, dining room and kitchen are separated only by a work island.

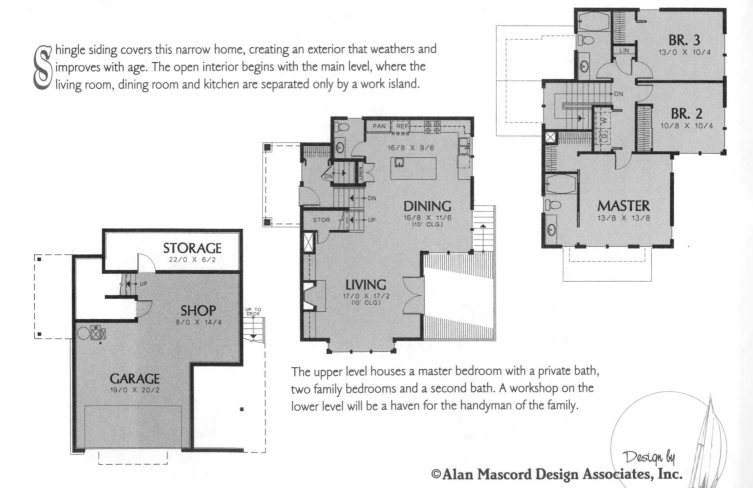

STORAGE
22/0 X 6/2

SHOP
8/0 X 14/4

UP

UP TO DECK

GARAGE
19/0 X 20/2

PAN   REF

16/8 X 9/6

DN

LINEN

DN

STOR

UP

DINING
16/8 X 11/6
(10' CLG.)

LIVING
17/0 X 17/2
(10' CLG.)

BR. 3
13/0 X 10/4

LIN

DN

BR. 2
10/8 X 10/4

W   D

MASTER
13/8 X 13/8

The upper level houses a master bedroom with a private bath, two family bedrooms and a second bath. A workshop on the lower level will be a haven for the handyman of the family.

Design by

©Alan Mascord Design Associates, Inc.

First Floor:
576 sq. ft.

Second Floor:
576 sq. ft.

Total:
1,152 sq. ft.

Width:
24'-0"

Depth:
24'-0"

This two-story home features a second-floor balcony to enjoy every view, from the mountains to the ocean. Large windows on each side of this home also allow for marvelous views of the outdoors. On the first floor the kitchen is open to the living area and just around the corner is a hall bath. Upstairs, the master bedroom offers a walk-in closet and full bath with a corner tub and separate shower. This home is designed with a basement foundation.

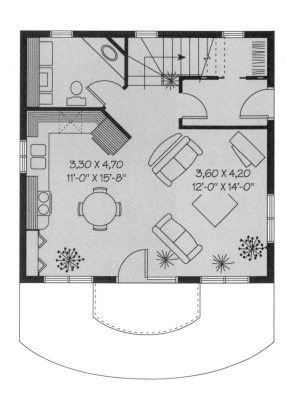

3,30 X 4,70
11'-0" X 15'-8"

3,60 X 4,20
12'-0" X 14'-0"

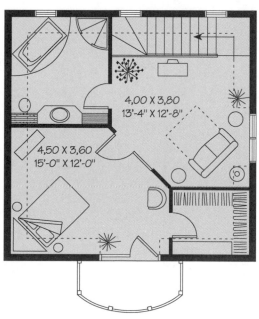

4,00 X 3,80
13'-4" X 12'-8"

4,50 X 3,60
15'-0" X 12'-0"

Design by
©Drummond Designs, Inc.

Design 7516

First Floor:
913 sq. ft.

Second Floor:
811 sq. ft.

Total:
1,724 sq. ft.

Width:
38'-0"

Depth:
33'-6"

Here's a charming country home that features elements of bungalow and farmhouse styles. An open living and dining area with a fireplace opens from the entry. Off the dining room, double doors open to a side porch—an inviting place for guests to linger and watch sunlight play on the water. A convenient powder room and a coat closet are thoughtfully placed in this area. The gourmet kitchen has a food prep counter and a walk-through pantry. Upstairs, the sleeping quarters include a main suite with a walk-in closet and separate lavatories, as well as two secondary bedrooms. The lower floor provides additional storage space and a service entrance from the garage.

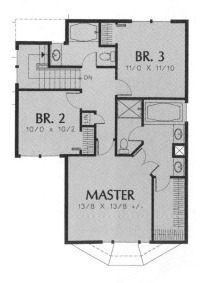

BR. 3
11/0 X 11/10

BR. 2
10/0 x 10/2

MASTER
13/8 X 13/8 +/-

STORAGE
10/2 X 10/8 +

STORAGE
8/0 x 10/0

GARAGE
19/0 x 24/0

PAN

DINING
14/6 x 10/2
(10' CLG.)

REF

LIVING
17/0 x 16/0 +/-
(10' CLG.)

Design by

©**Alan Mascord Design Associates, Inc.**

Design 7507

First Floor: 1,765 sq. ft.

Second Floor: 907 sq. ft.

Total: 2,672 sq. ft.

Width: 65'-0"

Depth: 42'-6"

This stunning facade is ready for an ocean view or a beautiful suburb. Two-story windows with transoms allow natural light to fill the great room, which opens to the formal dining room. A grand kitchen has wrapping counters and a morning nook opening to a terrace. The upper-level master suite provides a double-bowl vanity, a walk-in closet and a fireplace. A nearby den boasts its own fireplace and plenty of space for computers and books. The lower-level four-car garage offers additional storage.

Design by
© Alan Mascord Design Associates, Inc.

Design
6693

First Floor:
1,642 sq. ft.

Second Floor:
1,165 sq. ft.

Lower Floor:
150 sq. ft.

Total:
2,957 sq. ft.

Width:
44'-6"

Depth:
58'-0"

A faux widow's walk creates a stunning complement to the observation balcony and two sun decks. Inside, the open living and dining area is defined by two pairs of French doors that frame a two-story wall of glass, and built-ins flank the living-room fireplace. The efficient kitchen features a walk-in pantry, a work island, and a door to the covered porch. Split sleeping quarters offer privacy to the first-floor master suite. Upstairs, two guest suites both include private baths. A gallery loft leads to a computer area with a built-in desk and a balcony overlook.

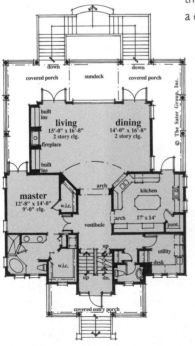

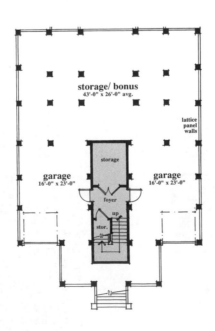

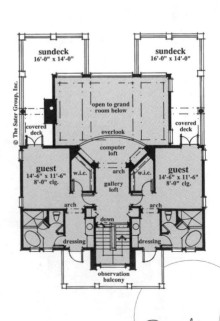

Design by
©The Sater Design Collection

Design
6692

Square Footage:
2,190

Width:
58'-0"

Depth:
54'-0"

The dramatic arched entry of this Southampton-style cottage borrows freely from its Southern coastal past. The foyer and central hall open to the grand room. The kitchen is flanked by the dining room and morning nook, which opens to the lanai. On the left side of the plan, the master suite also accesses the lanai. Two walk-in closets, a compartmented bath with separate tub and shower and a double-bowl vanity complete the homeowners' opulent retreat. The right side of the plan includes two secondary bedrooms and a full bath.

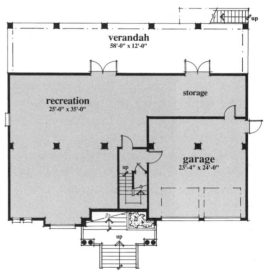

verandah
58'-0" x 12'-0"

recreation
25'-0" x 35'-0"

storage

garage
23'-4" x 24'-0"

©The Sater Group, Inc.

lanai
58'-0" x 10'-8"

master suite
13'-0" x 15'-0"
9'-4" stepped clg.

built ins

nook
11'-0" x 9'-4"

br. 2
12'-0" x 11'-4"
9'-4" flat clg.

grand room
20'-0" x 18'-0" avg.
tray ceiling

fireplace

built ins

kitchen
11' x 11'

eating bar

arch

arch

utility

hers

his

arch

foyer

down

dining
10'-10" x 15'-0"
9'-4" flat clg.

br. 3
12'-0" x 11'-0"
9'-4" flat clg.

study
11'-0" x 11'-0"
9'-4" flat clg.

dn.

entry porch

planter

Front View

Design
HPT7230004

First Floor:
1,855 sq. ft.

Second Floor:
901 sq. ft.

Total:
2,756 sq. ft.

Width:
66'-0"

Depth:
50'-0"

This Southern Tidewater cottage is the perfect vacation hideaway—easily blending into the seaside scenery. The wraparound entry porch is relaxing and inviting. Double doors open into the foyer—the study with built-in cabinetry is placed to the right and the formal dining room is to the left. An octagonal great room with a multi-faceted vaulted ceiling illuminates the interior. This room boasts a fireplace, a built-in entertainment center and three sets of double doors, which lead outside to a vaulted lanai. The island kitchen is brightened by a bumped-out window and a pass-through to the lanai. Two walk-in closets and a whirlpool bath await to indulge the homeowner in the master suite. Two additional family bedrooms are offered with private baths. A computer center and a morning kitchen complete the upstairs before opening to the outer deck.

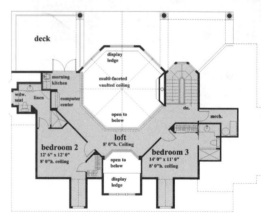

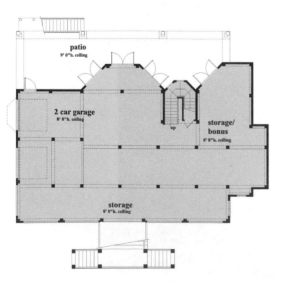

© The Sater Design Collection

Design by

Design
6684

Main Level:
2,385 sq. ft.

Lower Level:
80 sq. ft.

Total:
2,465 sq. ft.

Width:
60'-4"

Depth:
59'-4"

Front View

Adapted from styles found in the tropics and the Caribbean, this cottage plan is distinguished by its open porches, abundant windows and heavy overhangs. The lower level of the interior includes the garage and two rooms that could be used as storage space, recreation rooms or extra bedrooms. Upstairs, the great room offers an entertainment center, an eating bar and an adjacent breakfast nook. The master suite boasts a compartmented bath and two walk-in closets. On the opposite side of the plan are two family bedrooms, a full bath and a utility room.

covered porch
60'-4" x 10'-4"

storage/game room
33'-4" x 22'-4"

garage
25'-0" x 33'-4"

opt. elev.

storage

storage/bonus room
20'-0" x 16'-4"

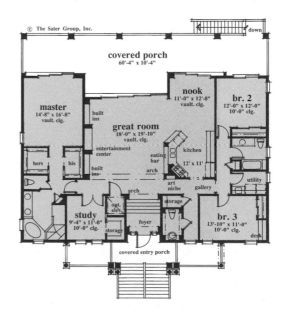

© The Sater Group, Inc.

down

covered porch
60'-4" x 10'-4"

master
14'-8" x 16'-8"
vault. clg.

built ins

nook
11'-0" x 12'-8"
vault. clg.

br. 2
12'-0" x 12'-0"
10'-0" clg.

great room
18'-0" x 19'-10"
vault. clg.

entertainment center

eating bar

kitchen
12' x 11'

hers

his

built ins

arch

utility

art niche

gallery

arch

study
9'-4" x 11'-0"
10'-0" clg.

opt. elev.

storage

storage

br. 3
13'-10" x 11'-0"
10'-0" clg.

foyer

desk

covered entry porch

Design by
©The Sater Design Collection

Design 6689

First Floor:
1,642 sq. ft.

Second Floor:
1,165 sq. ft.

Lower Floor:
150 sq. ft.

Total:
2,957 sq. ft.

Width:
44'-6"

Depth:
58'-0"

Prevailing summer breezes find their way through many joyful rooms in this Neoclassical Revival design. Inspired by 19th-Century Key West houses, the exterior is heart-stoppingly beautiful with Doric columns, lattice and fretwork, and a glass-paneled, arched entry. The mid-level foyer eases the trip from ground level to living and dining areas, which offer flexible space for planned events or cozy gatherings. Two sets of French doors lead out to the gallery and sun deck, and a two-story picture window invites natural light.

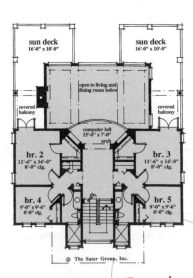

Front View

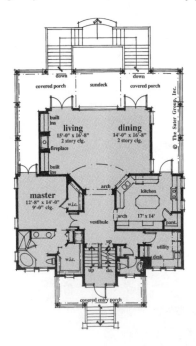

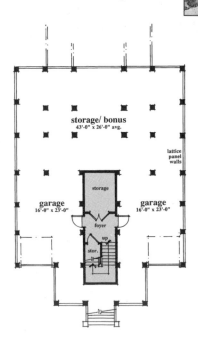

© The Sater Group, Inc.

©The Sater Design Collection

Design by

First Floor:
637 sq. ft.

Second Floor:
1,022 sq. ft.

Total:
2,659 sq. ft.

Bonus Space:
532 sq. ft.

Width:
50'-0"

Depth:
53'-0"

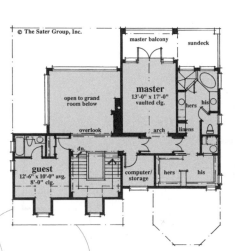

Front View

Variable rooflines, a tower and a covered front porch all combine to give this home a wonderful ambiance. Enter through the mid-level foyer and head either up to the main living level or down to the garage. On the main level, find a spacious, light-filled great room sharing a fireplace with the dining room. A study offers access to the rear covered veranda. The efficient island kitchen is open to the dining room, offering ease in entertaining. A guest suite with a private full bath completes this level. Upstairs, a second guest room with its own bath and a deluxe master suite with a covered balcony, sun deck, walk-in closet and lavish bath are sure to please.

© The Sater Group, Inc.

master balcony

sundeck

open to grand room below

master
13'-0" x 17'-0"
vaulted clg.

hers **his**

overlook **arch** **linens**

guest
12'-6" x 10'-0" avg.
8'-0" clg.

dn.

computer/ storage **hers** **his**

© The Sater Group, Inc.

covered veranda
50'-0" x 10'-0" avg.

serving bar

corner fireplace **dining**
12'-6" x 15'-0"
9'-0" clg.

kitchen

great room
15'-0" x 16'-0"
18'-4" clg.

eating bar

11' x 15'

entertainment center

gallery **art niche**

study
12'-6" x 15'-0"
9'-0" clg.

dn. **up** **utility**

mid level foyer

covered entry porch

guest
15'-0" x 14'-6"
9'-0" clg.

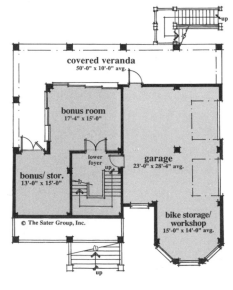

up

dn.

covered veranda
50'-0" x 10'-0" avg.

bonus room
17'-4" x 15'-0"

garage
23'-0" x 28'-4" avg.

bonus/ stor.
13'-0" x 15'-0"

lower foyer

up

© The Sater Group, Inc.

bike storage/ workshop
15'-0" x 14'-0" avg.

up

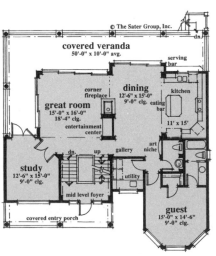

Design by
© **The Sater Design Collection**

Design
A262

First Floor:
1,824 sq. ft.

Second Floor:
842 sq. ft.

Total:
2,666 sq. ft.

Width:
59'-0"

Depth:
53'-6"

Horizontal siding, double-hung windows and European gables lend a special charm to this contemporary home. The formal dining room opens from the foyer and offers a servery and a box-bay window. The great room features a fireplace and opens to a golf porch as well as a charming side porch. A well-lit kitchen has a cooktop island counter and two pantries.

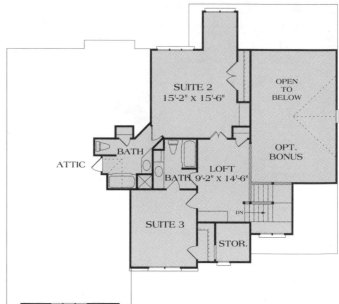

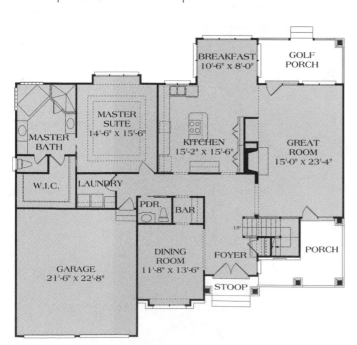

The first-floor master suite has a tray ceiling, a box-bay window and a deluxe bath with a garden tub and an angled shower. A convenient powder room maintains privacy for the master suite. Each of the upper-level bedrooms has private access to a full bath. Suite 2 has a dormer window and leads to sizable attic space.

Design by

©Living Concepts Home Planning

Design
6688

First Floor:
1,293 sq. ft.

Second Floor:
1,154 sq. ft.

Total:
2,447 sq. ft.

Bonus Room:
426 sq. ft.

Width:
50'-0"

Depth:
90'-0"

Rear View

T his home is a water-lover's dream. Spend long summer hours on the sun deck and in the pool and spa, surrounded by fountains and planters. The covered porch and balcony offer additional outdoor retreats. Distinctive arches, sturdy columns and cornice detailing characterize the exterior. To the right of the entry foyer are the study and powder room; to the left are the kitchen and formal living areas. The dining room opens to the kitchen through archways. Arches also accent the threshold to the great room, where the main interest is an unusual curved window. Upstairs, a second curved window accents the master suite, which also features double doors and two walk-in closets.

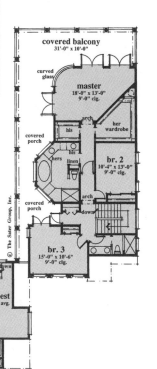

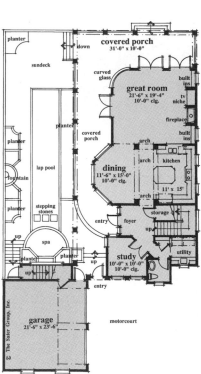

Design by
©The Sater Design Collection

Design E148

First Floor:
731 sq. ft.

Second Floor:
935 sq. ft.

Look Out:
138 sq. ft.

Total:
1,804 sq. ft.

Width:
34'-0"

Depth:
26'-0"

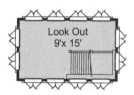

Look Out
9'x 15'

Perfect for a seaside abode, this pier-foundation home has an abundance of amenities to offer, not the least being the loft look-out. Here, with a 360-degree view, one can watch the storms come in over the water, or gaze with wonder on the colors of the sea. Inside the home just off the screened porch, the living room is complete with a corner gas fireplace. The spacious kitchen features a cooktop island, an adjacent breakfast nook and easy access to the dining room. From this room, a set of French doors lead out to a small deck—perfect for dining alfresco. Upstairs, the sleeping zone consists of two family bedrooms sharing a full hall bath, and a deluxe master suite. Amenities here include two walk-in closets and a private bath.

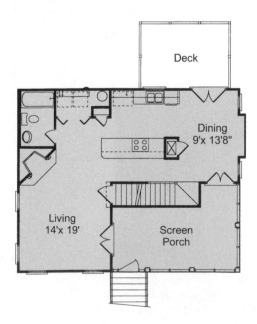

Deck

Dining
9'x 13'8"

Living
14'x 19'

Screen
Porch

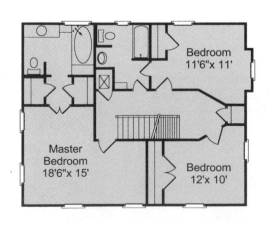

Bedroom
11'6"x 11'

Master
Bedroom
18'6"x 15'

Bedroom
12'x 10'

Design by

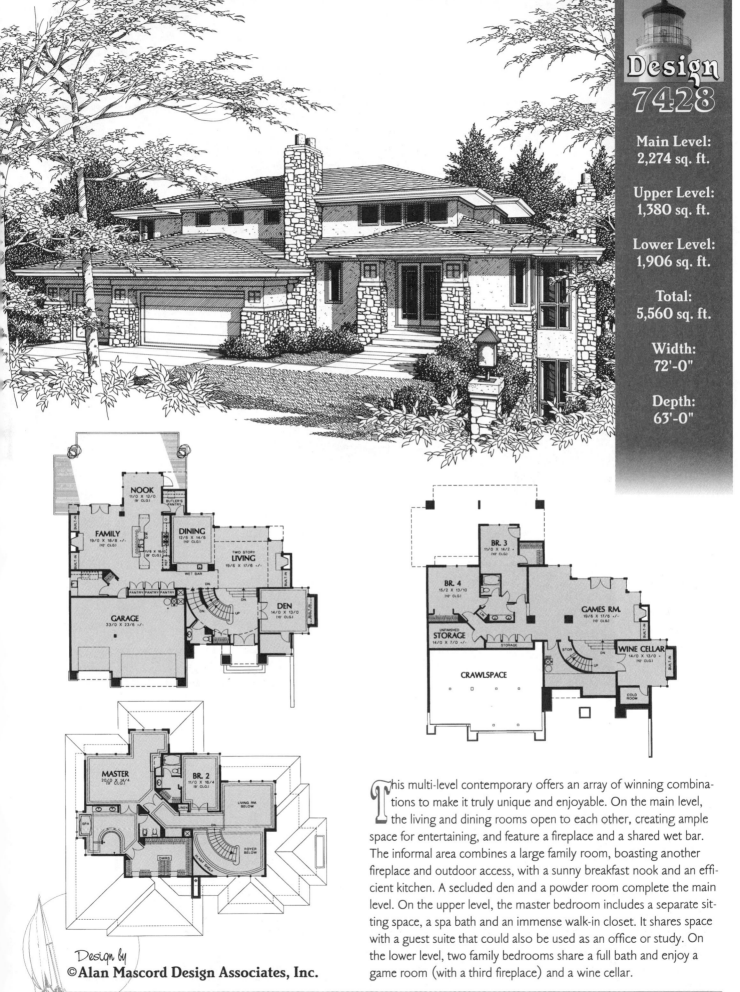

Design by
© Alan Mascord Design Associates, Inc.

Design 7428

Main Level:
2,274 sq. ft.

Upper Level:
1,380 sq. ft.

Lower Level:
1,906 sq. ft.

Total:
5,560 sq. ft.

Width:
72'-0"

Depth:
63'-0"

NOOK
11/0 X 12/0
[9' CLG.]

BUTLER'S PANTRY

FAMILY
19/0 X 18/8 +/-
[10' CLG.]

DINING
12/6 X 14/6
[10' CLG.]

TWO STORY
LIVING
19/6 X 17/6 +/-
[9' CLG.]

WET BAR

PANTRY PANTRY PANTRY

DEN
14/0 X 13/0
[10' CLG.]

GARAGE
33/0 X 23/6 +/-

BR. 3
11/0 X 14/2
[10' CLG.]

BR. 4
15/2 X 13/10
[10' CLG.]

GAMES RM.
19/6 X 17/6 +/-
[10' CLG.]

UNFINISHED
STORAGE
14/0 X 7/0 +/-

STORAGE

WINE CELLAR
14/0 X 13/0
[10' CLG.]

CRAWLSPACE

COLD ROOM

MASTER
20/0 X 14/4
[9' CLG.]

BR. 2
11/0 X 16/4
[9' CLG.]

SPA

LIVING RM.
BELOW

LINEN

DWRS

PLANT SHELF

FOYER
BELOW

This multi-level contemporary offers an array of winning combinations to make it truly unique and enjoyable. On the main level, the living and dining rooms open to each other, creating ample space for entertaining, and feature a fireplace and a shared wet bar. The informal area combines a large family room, boasting another fireplace and outdoor access, with a sunny breakfast nook and an efficient kitchen. A secluded den and a powder room complete the main level. On the upper level, the master bedroom includes a separate sitting space, a spa bath and an immense walk-in closet. It shares space with a guest suite that could also be used as an office or study. On the lower level, two family bedrooms share a full bath and enjoy a game room (with a third fireplace) and a wine cellar.

Design 7627

First Floor:
1,514 sq. ft.

Second Floor:
642 sq. ft.

Total:
2,156 sq. ft.

Width:
64'-4"

Depth:
46'-4"

Sleek contemporary lines from the rugged Northwest coast, plenty of windows and a combination of textures give this home a lot of curb appeal. Great for entertaining, the formal dining room has a pass-through to the kitchen for ease in serving. The adjacent great room offers a fireplace, built-ins and access to both the rear deck and the sun room. Located on the first floor for privacy, the master suite features many luscious amenities. Two bedrooms, a full bath and a loft complete the second floor.

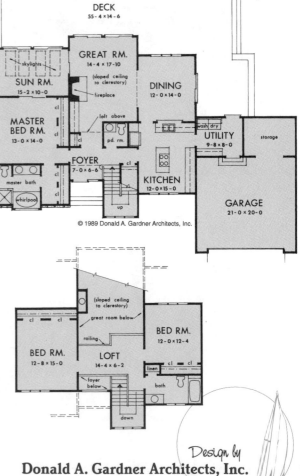

Front View

Design by

Donald A. Gardner Architects, Inc.

First Floor:
1,657 sq. ft.

Second Floor:
845 sq. ft.

Total:
2,502 sq. ft.

Width:
62'-0"

Depth:
57'-4"

Find a sunny spot to relax in this Northwest coastal contemporary design—it isn't hard as there are sun-filled rooms everywhere. It begins with the dining room with a wall of windows. Continue to the family room with an attached sun room and an octagonal breakfast room. Even the living room allows passage to a rear deck. Two bedrooms on the first floor share a full bath. Upstairs, the master suite offers a sun room/balcony. The study overlooks the living room and leads to an additional bedroom with full bath.

DECK
33 - 6 × 10 - 0

spa

SUN RM.
14 - 0 × 8 - 10

LIVING RM.
13 - 4 × 18 - 10

fireplace

FAMILY RM.
12 - 0 × 12 - 4

fireplace

BRKFST.
8 - 8 × 9 - 0

study above

storage

BED RM.
10 - 6 × 11 - 8

cl

KITCHEN
19 - 4 × 8 - 4

FOYER
9 - 10 × 10 - 4

bath

cl

wash dry

storage

UTILITY
9 - 4 × 6 - 0

DINING
14 - 0 × 12 - 0

cl

up

BED RM.
10 - 6 × 12 - 0

cl

GARAGE
20 - 4 × 20 - 0

© 1989 Donald A. Gardner Architects, Inc.

open to sun room below

SUN RM. BALCONY

(sloped ceiling to clerestory)

living room below

MASTER BED RM.
14 - 0 × 14 - 6

fireplace

railing

bath

cl

clerestory above

STUDY
9 - 10 × 7 - 8

BED RM.
10 - 6 × 10 - 6

walk-in closet

foyer below

down

master bath

lin.

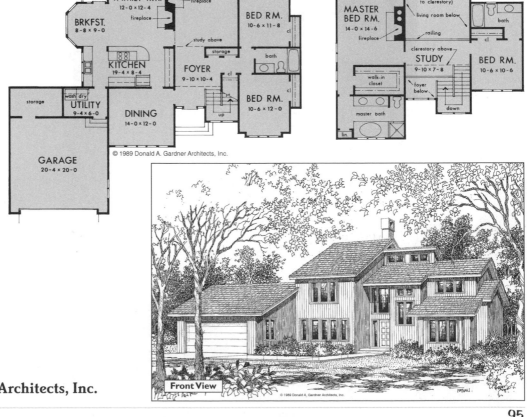

Front View

© 1989 Donald A. Gardner Architects, Inc.

Design by
Donald A. Gardner Architects, Inc.

Design A239

First Floor:
774 sq. ft.

Second Floor:
723 sq. ft.

Total:
1,497 sq. ft.

Width:
42'-0"

Depth:
43'-0"

DECK / PATIO

LAUN.

GARAGE
19'-8" x 21'-0"

KITCHEN
7'-6" x 14'-0"

GATHERING ROOM
14'-0" x 21'-0"

PANT.

PDR.

DINING ROOM
8'-8" x 12'-0"

FOYER

UP

PORCH

MASTER SUITE
15'-0" x 12'-0"

MASTER BATH

SUITE 2
11'-0" x 9'-6"

W.I.C.

BATH

LIN.

DN

SUITE 3
10'-0" x 10'-6"

OPEN TO BELOW

PLANT LEDGE

Shingles and siding combine to give this home a fine coastal feeling. The spacious gathering room has a fireplace and a French door to the back deck or patio. The L-shaped kitchen provides an ample pantry and plenty of counter space and has easy access to the formal dining room. A service entrance leads from the garage through the laundry room to the gathering room. The upper-level master suite has a walk-in closet, a double-bowl vanity and a garden tub. Two family bedrooms share a hall bath and complete this floor.

Design by

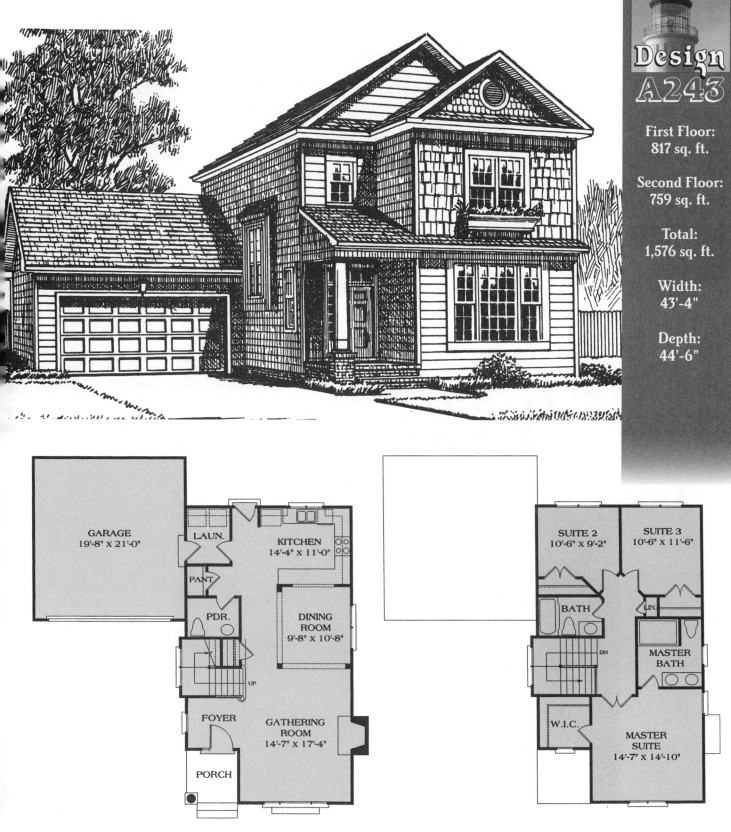

Design
A243

First Floor:
817 sq. ft.

Second Floor:
759 sq. ft.

Total:
1,576 sq. ft.

Width:
43'-4"

Depth:
44'-6"

GARAGE
19'-8" x 21'-0"

LAUN.

KITCHEN
14'-4" x 11'-0"

PANT

PDR.

DINING
ROOM
9'-8" x 10'-8"

UP

FOYER

GATHERING
ROOM
14'-7" x 17'-4"

PORCH

SUITE 2
10'-6" x 9'-2"

SUITE 3
10'-6" x 11'-6"

BATH

LIN.

DN

MASTER
BATH

W.I.C.

MASTER
SUITE
14'-7" x 14'-10"

An open-plan layout gives this design maximum livability. The spacious gathering room, just past the entry foyer, is given interest by a fireplace and flows into the dining area separated from the living area by decorative columns. A powder room, U-shaped kitchen and laundry complete the main level. Sleeping quarters on the second floor include two family bedrooms and a master suite with a walk-in closet and private bath. The two-car garage easily shelters the family fleet.

Design by
© **Living Concepts Home Planning**

Design 3522

D

First Floor:
1,267 sq. ft.

Second Floor:
833 sq. ft.

Total:
2,100 sq. ft.

Width:
41'-6"

Depth:
47'-6"

DINING

PORCH

GATHERING ROOM
14⁰ X 19⁰
9'-0" CEILING

RAISED HEARTH

KIT
11⁸ X 13⁶
9'-0" CEILING

P

SINK   DW

COOK TOP

LAUND

REF'S

OVEN

W

D

SHLVS

SHLVS

FOYER
9'-0" CLG

PDR

UP

DN

COVERED PORCH

BUILT-INS

LIBRARY
19⁰ X 14⁰
9'-0" CEILING

BUILT-INS   BUILT-INS

WINDOW SEAT

MASTER SUITE
14⁸ X 14⁰

CEILING CLIP

GARDEN TUB

S

LOW WALL

MASTER BATH

LINEN LINEN

BATH

HALL

RAILING

DN

BEDRM
14⁰ X 11⁸

CEILING CLIP

Quote One®

Cost to build? See page 198
to order complete cost estimate
to build this house in your area!

A quiet cottage—bringing to life the charm of a bygone era, this 1½-story plan contains a commodious floor plan. The covered porch leads to a side-facing entry opening to a large, open foyer. To the front of the plan is the library with built-ins and a bay-window seat. The kitchen and gathering room—with its beamed ceiling and fireplace—are to the rear of the plan. Notice the dining space in a windowed nook. Upstairs are two bedrooms and two full baths. The master suite has a walk-in closet and well-appointed bath.

Design by
©Home Planners

Design
2493

First Floor:
1,387 sq. ft.

Second Floor:
929 sq. ft.

Total:
2,316 sq. ft.

Width:
30'-0"

Depth:
51'-8"

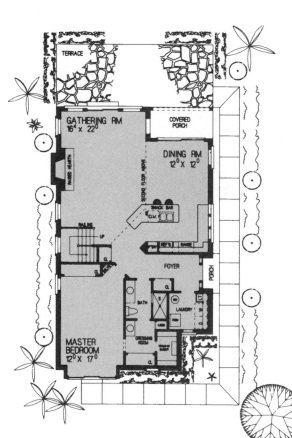

Perfect for a narrow lot, this shingle-and stone-sided Nantucket Cape caters to the casual lifestyle. The side entrance gives direct access to the wonderfully open living areas: gathering room with fireplace; kitchen with angled, pass-through snack bar; dining area with sliding glass doors to a covered eating area. Note also the large deck that further extends the living potential. Also on this floor is a large master suite. Upstairs is a convenient guest suite with private balcony. It is complemented by two smaller bedrooms.

QUOTE ONE®
Cost to build? See page 198
to order complete cost estimate
to build this house in your area!

Design by
©Home Planners

Design T187

Square Footage: 2,721

Width: 69'-3"

Depth: 79'-3"

© American Home Gallery, Ltd.

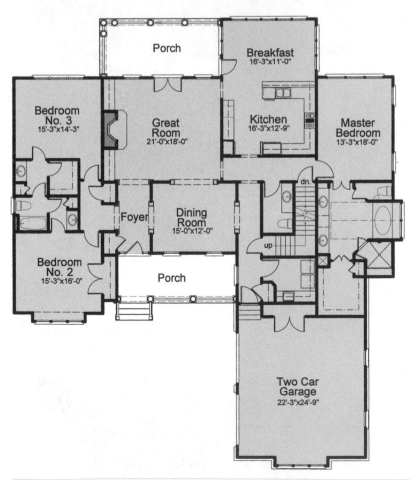

Porch

Breakfast
16'-3"x11'-0"

Bedroom No. 3
15'-3"x14'-3"

Great Room
21'-0"x18'-0"

Kitchen
16'-3"x12'-9"

Master Bedroom
13'-3"x18'-0"

dn.

Foyer

Dining Room
15'-0"x12'-0"

up

Bedroom No. 2
15'-3"x16'-0"

Porch

Two Car Garage
22'-3"x24'-9"

In this design, equally at home in the country or at the coast, classic elements play against a rustic shingle-and-stone exterior. Doric porch columns provide the elegance, while banks of cottage-style windows let in lots of natural light. The symmetrical layout of the foyer and formal dining room blend easily with the cozy great room. Here, a fireplace creates a welcome atmosphere that invites you to select a novel from one of the built-in bookcases and curl up in your favorite easy chair. The adjacent U-shaped kitchen combines with a sunny breakfast room that opens onto a rear porch, making casual meals a pleasure. Split away from family bedrooms for privacy, the master suite occupies the right side of the house and enjoys a dramatic master bath. The left wing contains two secondary bedrooms that share a bath with compartmented vanity/dressing areas. This home is designed with a basement foundation.

Design by
Stephen Fuller

Square Footage: 1,288

Width: 32'-4"

Depth: 60'-0"

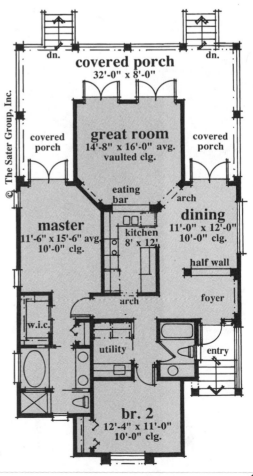

© The Sater Group, Inc.

covered porch 32'-0" x 8'-0"

dn. dn.

covered porch

great room 14'-8" x 16'-0" avg. vaulted clg.

covered porch

eating bar

arch

master 11'-6" x 15'-6" avg. 10'-0" clg.

kitchen 8' x 12'

dining 11'-0" x 12'-0" 10'-0" clg.

half wall

w.i.c.

arch

foyer

utility

entry

br. 2 12'-4" x 11'-0" 10'-0" clg.

Front View

Welcome home to casual, unstuffy living with this comfortable tidewater design. Asymmetrical lines celebrate the turn of the new century, and blend a current Gulf Coast style with vintage panache brought forward from its regional past. The heart of this home is the great room, where a put-your-feet-up atmosphere prevails, and the dusky hues of sunset can mingle with the sounds of ocean breakers. French doors open the master suite to a private area of the covered porch, where sunlight and sea breezes mingle with a spirit of quiet joy.

Design by
©**The Sater Design Collection**

Design
Z216

First Floor:
822 sq. ft.

Second Floor:
400 sq. ft.

Observatory:
32 sq. ft.

Total:
1,254 sq. ft.

Width:
62'-0"

Depth:
28'-4"

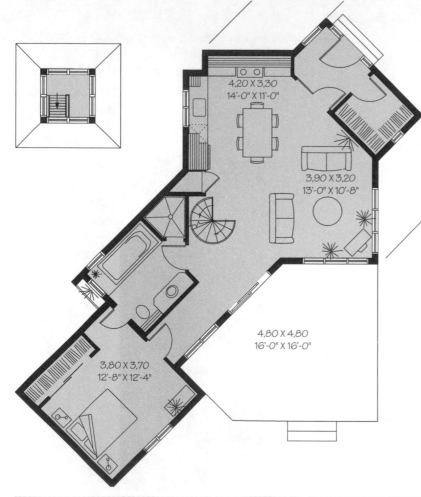

4,20 X 3,30
14'-0" X 11'-0"

3,90 X 3,20
13'-0" X 10'-8"

4,80 X 4,80
16'-0" X 16'-0"

3,80 X 3,70
12'-8" X 12'-4"

An observatory and private master bedroom add appeal to this unique seaside home. The first floor has an open floor plan that combines the family room with the eat-in kitchen where counter and cabinet space abounds. The master bedroom suite is tucked away for privacy and has direct access to a full bathroom. A charming spiral staircase leads upstairs to a second bedroom—or make it a study—which offers access to the unique observatory. Accenting the abundance of windows on the lower floors, the observatory is also perfect for panoramic views.

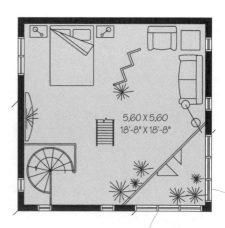

5,60 X 5,60
18'-8" X 18'-8"

Design by

©**Drummond Designs, Inc.**

Design
V004

Square
Footage:
2,927

Width:
93'-4"

Depth:
60'-7"

This is truly a light-filled design—with full and transom windows in many of the interior spaces to give a feeling of connectedness to the outdoors. Double doors open directly to the foyer. At the right is a study with double closets. Ahead is the formal dining area, separated from the spacious great room by a through-fireplace. This room offers a unique shape, echoing the prow of a ship at one end. The island kitchen has an attached nook and nearby powder room. The full-width deck to the rear of the plan can be reached from the dining area, the great room and the master bedroom. Family bedrooms share a full bath with dual sinks. The master bedroom boasts a private bath with garden tub and walk-in closet.

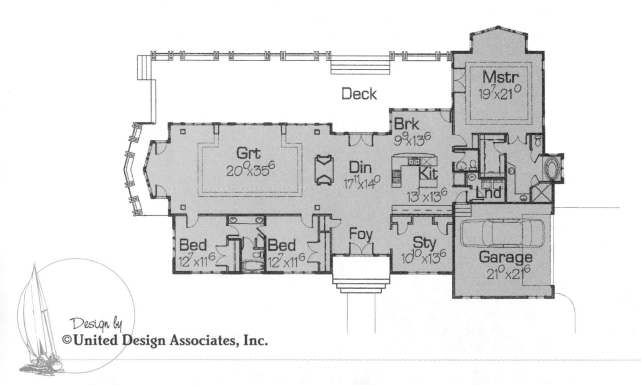

Deck

Mstr
19⁷x21⁰

Brk
9⁹x13⁶

Grt
20⁰x35⁶

Din
17¹¹x14⁰

Kit
13⁰x13⁶

Lnd

Bed
12⁷x11⁶

Bed
12⁷x11⁶

Foy

Sty
10¹⁰x13⁶

Garage
21⁰x21⁶

Design by
©United Design Associates, Inc.

Design 6686

First Floor:
1,046 sq. ft.

Second Floor:
638 sq. ft.

Total:
1,684 sq. ft.

Width:
25'-0"

Depth:
65'-6"

A Key West design that can be built anywhere, this cozy three-bedroom home has plenty to offer. Built-ins and a media niche frame the fireplace in the great room, creating a cozy complement to the beautiful views from the wraparound covered porch. The formal dining room also opens to the porch and features direct access to the U-shaped island kitchen. A secondary bedroom on this floor has a nearby full bath. The second level is dedicated to the master suite, where the bed wall faces the private observation deck. A sensible bath offers a walk-in closet, an over-sized shower and a compartmented toilet. A vestibule leads to a viewing-loft stair and to Bedroom 3, where a built-in window seat may be enjoyed.

Rear View

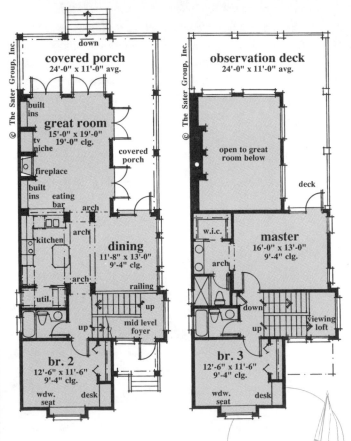

© The Sater Group, Inc.

covered porch
24'-0" x 11'-0" avg.

built-ins

great room
15'-0" x 19'-0"
19'-0" clg.

tv niche

fireplace

built-ins

eating bar

kitchen

arch

arch

arch

util.

dining
11'-8" x 13'-0"
9'-4" clg.

railing

up

up

mid level foyer

br. 2
12'-6" x 11'-6"
9'-4" clg.

wdw. seat

desk

© The Sater Group, Inc.

observation deck
24'-0" x 11'-0" avg.

open to great room below

deck

w.i.c.

master
16'-0" x 13'-0"
9'-4" clg.

arch

down

up

viewing loft

br. 3
12'-6" x 11'-6"
9'-4" clg.

wdw. seat

desk

down

Design by
©**The Sater Design Collection**

First Floor:
737 sq. ft.

Second Floor:
587 sq. ft.

Total:
1,324 sq. ft.

Width:
33'-0"

Depth:
26'-0"

2,40 X 2,70
8'-0" X 9'-0"

3,30 X 5,70
11'-0" X 19'-0"

4,20 X 4,80
14'-0" X 16'-0"

8,40 X 5,70
28'-0" X 19'-0"

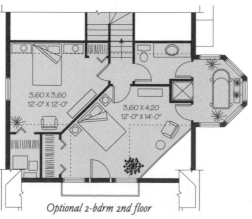

3,60 X 3,60
12'-0" X 12'-0"

3,60 X 4,20
12'-0" X 14'-0"

Optional 2-bdrm 2nd floor

This home is absolutely full of windows, and a large deck enhances the outdoor living possibilities. Picture the wall of windows facing the seashore, with the sound of waves lulling you into a calm, comfortable feeling. Inside, an open floor plan includes a family/dining room, an L-shaped kitchen with snack bar, and a full bath with laundry facilities. A special treat is the bumped-out hot tub room, almost entirely surrounded by windows. Upstairs, choose either the one or two bedroom plan. Both include a full bath and access to the upper balcony. This home is designed with a basement foundation.

Design by
©Drummond Designs, Inc.

Design T155

First Floor:
1,567 sq. ft.

Second Floor:
1,895 sq. ft.

Total:
3,462 sq. ft.

Width:
63'-0"

Depth:
53'-6"

© American Home Gallery, Ltd.

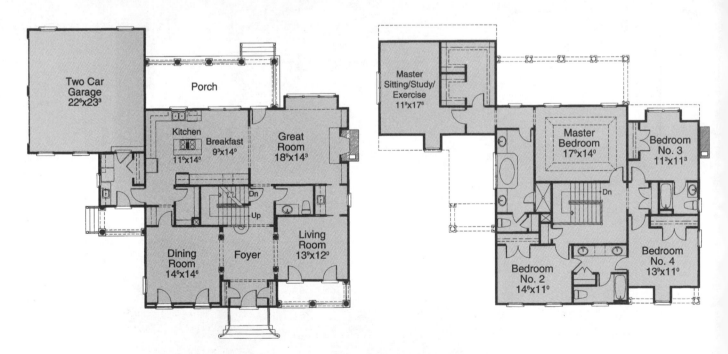

Two Car Garage 22⁶x23³

Porch

Kitchen 11⁰x14⁰

Breakfast 9³x14⁰

Great Room 18⁹x14³

Dining Room 14⁶x14⁶

Foyer

Living Room 13⁹x12⁰

Dn

Up

Master Sitting/Study/ Exercise 11⁹x17⁶

Master Bedroom 17⁹x14⁰

Bedroom No. 3 11³x11³

Dn

Bedroom No. 2 14⁶x11⁰

Bedroom No. 4 13⁹x11⁰

Although the facade looks like a seaside cottage, this home's fine proportions contain formal living areas, including dining and living rooms. At the back of the main level, you'll find a kitchen and breakfast nook. A great room with a fireplace and a bumped-out window provides comfort. Upstairs, four bedrooms include a master suite with lavish bath and a sitting room that could easily be converted to a study or exercise room. This home is designed with a basement foundation.

Design by
Stephen Fuller

LAKEFRONT LIVING

Homes designed for the Lakeshore

Design T186 by Stephen Fuller. See page 32 for details

"Down from

the line of

the shore's

deep shadows,

another and softer

picture lies—

As if the soul

of the lake

in slumber should

harbor a dream

of paradise."

Bliss Carman

Design F100

First Floor:
448 sq. ft.

Second Floor:
448 sq. ft.

Total:
896 sq. ft.

Width:
16'-0"

Depth:
28'-0"

This petite Carpenter Gothic charmer would make an ideal lakeside vacation home or a starter home for the young family. The exterior boasts a heavy wood-shingled roof, board-and-batten siding and decorative scroll-sawn rake detailing. The delicately bracketed but very practical porch provides seating space for relaxing on warm summer nights. A well planned interior is simplicity itself: a double-door entry opens to an all encompassing living, dining and kitchen area. The kitchen is hidden from the living room by a stairway and a half bath. Nine-foot ceilings highlight the second floor, which contains two family bedrooms—each with plenty of closet space—and a bathroom with a linen closet.

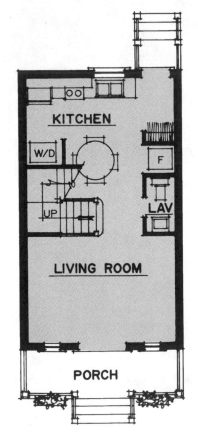

KITCHEN

W/D

F

UP

LAV

LIVING ROOM

PORCH

BEDROOM 2

LIN.

BATH

DN

BEDROOM 1

Design by
©R.L. Pfotenhauer

First Floor:
895 sq. ft.

Second Floor:
576 sq. ft.

Total:
1,471 sq. ft.

Width:
26'-0"

Depth:
36'-0"

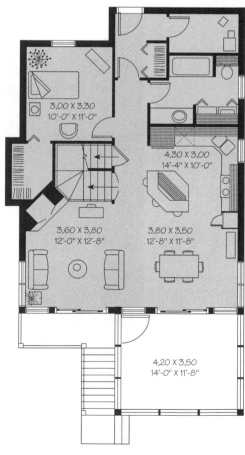

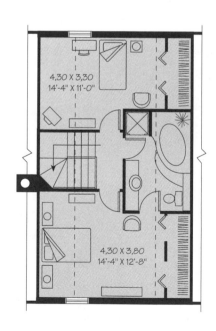

A lovely sun room opens from the dining room and allows great views of the nearby lake. An angled hearth warms the living and dining areas. The gourmet kitchen has an island counter with a snack bar. The main-level master bedroom enjoys a walk-in closet and a nearby bath. Two family bedrooms on the second floor share a full bath with a corner tub and a separate shower. A daylight basement allows a lower-level portico. This home is designed with a basement foundation.

4,30 X 3,30
14'-4" X 11'-0"

4,30 X 3,80
14'-4" X 12'-8"

3,00 X 3,30
10'-0" X 11'-0"

4,30 X 3,00
14'-4" X 10'-0"

3,60 X 3,80
12'-0" X 12'-8"

3,80 X 3,50
12'-8" X 11'-8"

4,20 X 3,50
14'-0" X 11'-8"

Design by
© **Drummond Designs, Inc.**

Design 2003

Main Level:
1,099 sq. ft.

Lower Level:
822 sq. ft.

Total:
1,921 sq. ft.

Width:
60'-0"

Depth:
39'-0"

With its wide windows and wraparound porch, this traditional design is ideal for a site with splendid lakeside views. Families will also enjoy special features designed with teenagers in mind. On the lower level they will find two bedrooms—each with a private bathroom—access to a private patio, plus their own living area on the main level (stairs are located in front of their rooms). Direct access to a shower and toilet from the backyard make this home perfect for outdoor pursuits. There are gorgeous views from the main living room on the main level and the master suite on the lower level. Other features include a large covered porch on the ground level, a daylight basement and a two-car garage.

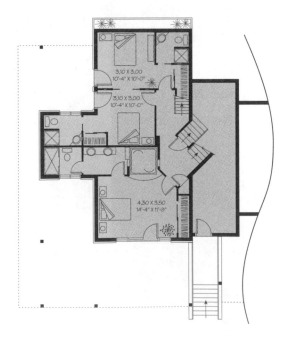

©Drummond Designs, Inc.

Design by

Design
Q292

First Floor:
1,036 sq. ft.

Second Floor:
630 sq. ft.

Total:
1,666 sq. ft.

Width:
45'-6"

Depth:
44'-0"

Stone and siding work in concert to complement this cozy design, with chalet features. The vaulted living and dining rooms, with exposed beam ceilings, are open to the loft above. A spacious wood storage area is found off the living room to feed the warm hearth inside. The kitchen features a pass-through counter to the dining area and leads to a laundry room with work bench. The master suite is on the first floor and has a private patio and bath. An additional half-bath is located in the main hall. The second floor holds a family room with desk and two family bedrooms with shared bath.

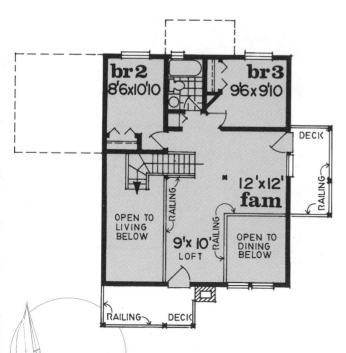

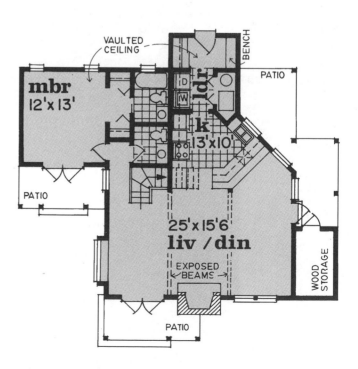

Design by
©Select Home Designs

Design
3842
3844

First Floor:
1,328 sq. ft.

Second Floor:
503 sq. ft.

Lower Floor:
403 sq. ft.

Total:
2,234/1,831 sq. ft.

Width:
44'-0"

Depth:
52'-0"

Design 3842

Expansive views enhance both floor plans of these fine retreats or lakeside homes. The difference is in the basement offered with Design 3842, raising the deck up one level. If you prefer to enjoy your sunrise and sunset from a ground-level deck, then Design 3844 is the perfect choice for you. Thoughtful planning creates open, flowing spaces on the main level. Here, a living room warmed by a fireplace shares space with an efficient eating nook and kitchen. Two bedrooms—one a master suite—complete this level. The upper level contains two family bedrooms, a full bath and an open loft that overlooks the main-level living room. If Design 3842 is chosen, the lower level includes a large basement area, a full bath and a covered patio.

Design 3844

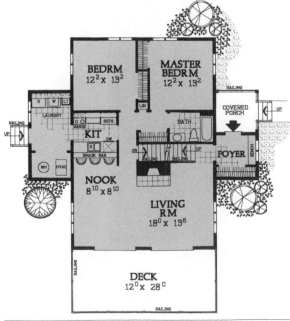

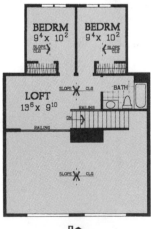

Lower Level Floor Plan

QUOTE ONE®
Cost to build? See page 198
to order complete cost estimate
to build this house in your area!

Design by
©Home Planners

Design Q508

First Floor:
1,296 sq. ft.

Second Floor:
396 sq. ft.

Total:
1,692 sq. ft.

Width:
55'-6"

Depth:
33'-0"

br2
9'2x10'4

br3
9'1x10'4

mbr
13'2x11'4

DN
RAILING
up

din
10'x11'4

K
10'x11'4

W.
D
F.
R.

liv
21'x14'6
VAULTED

DECK

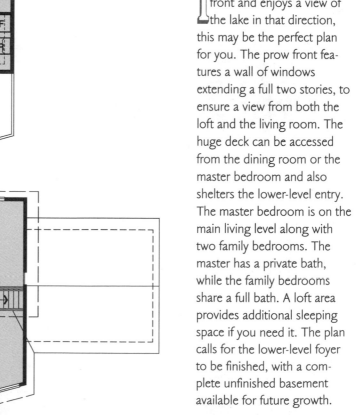

loft
21'0x17'6

RAILING

DN

OPEN TO
BELOW

If your lot slopes to the front and enjoys a view of the lake in that direction, this may be the perfect plan for you. The prow front features a wall of windows extending a full two stories, to ensure a view from both the loft and the living room. The huge deck can be accessed from the dining room or the master bedroom and also shelters the lower-level entry. The master bedroom is on the main living level along with two family bedrooms. The master has a private bath, while the family bedrooms share a full bath. A loft area provides additional sleeping space if you need it. The plan calls for the lower-level foyer to be finished, with a complete unfinished basement available for future growth.

Design by
©Select Home Designs

Design N126

First Floor:
1,016 sq. ft.

Second Floor:
400 sq. ft.

Total:
1,416 sq. ft.

Width:
24'-0"

Depth:
44'-4"

This cleverly modified A-frame combines a dramatic exterior with an exciting interior, which offers a commanding view through its vast expanse of windows. The central foyer leads to the spacious living/dining room on the left, with a soaring cathedral ceiling and stone fireplace. Ahead is a kitchen with sliding glass doors opening to the wraparound deck. In the rear are two bedrooms and a bath, with another bedroom and bath upstairs. The broad balcony overlooking the living room can serve as a lounge or extra guest room. Natural wood siding and shingles and plank flooring add to the rustic effect.

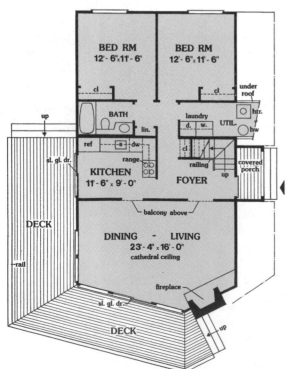

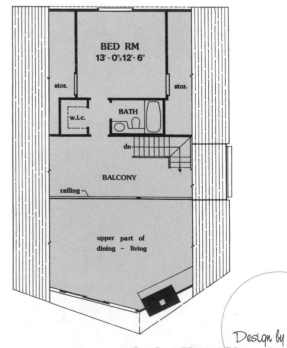

© **Perfect Home Plans, Inc.**

Design Q424

First Floor:
898 sq. ft.

Second Floor:
358 sq. ft.

Total:
1,256 sq. ft.

Width:
34'-0"

Depth:
32'-0"

A surrounding sun deck and expansive window wall capitalize on lakeside views in this design. The full-height windows flood the living and dining rooms with abundant natural light and bring attention to the high vaulted ceilings. A wood stove in the living area warms cold winter nights. The efficient U-shaped kitchen has ample counter and cupboard space. Behind it is a laundry room and rear entrance. The master bedroom sits on this floor and has a large wall closet and full bath. Two family bedrooms on the second floor have use of a half bath.

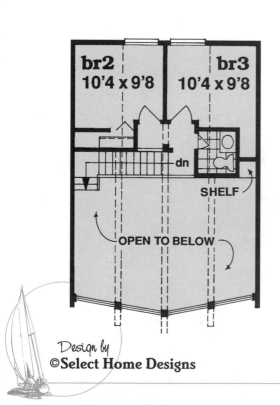

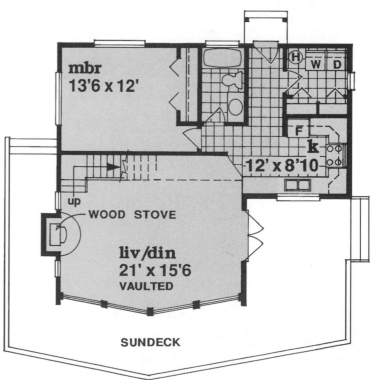

Design by
©Select Home Designs

Design
3658

LD

First Floor:
784 sq. ft.

Second Floor:
275 sq. ft.

Total:
1,059 sq. ft.

Width:
32'-0"

Depth:
30'-0"

This chalet-type vacation home, with its steep, overhanging roof, will catch the eye of even the most casual onlooker. It is designed to be completely livable, whether the season be for swimming or skiing. The dormitory on the upper level will sleep many vacationers, while the two bedrooms on the first floor pro- vide the more convenient and conventional sleeping facilities. The upper level overlooks the beam-ceilinged living and dining area. With a wraparound terrace and plenty of storage space, what more could you ask for?

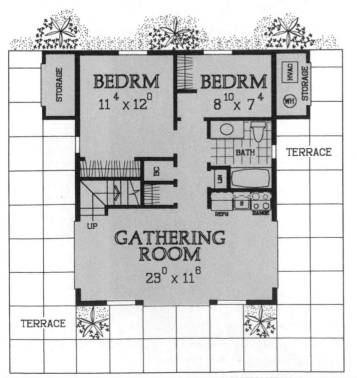

BEDRM
11⁴ x 12⁰

BEDRM
8¹⁰ x 7⁴

STORAGE

HVAC

STORAGE

WH

BATH

TERRACE

BC

LN

REFG   RANGE

UP

GATHERING ROOM
23⁰ x 11⁶

TERRACE

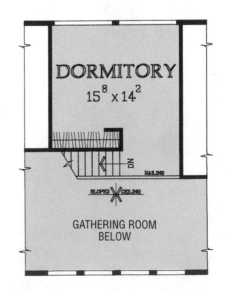

DORMITORY
15⁸ x 14²

DN

RAILING

SLOPED CEILING

GATHERING ROOM BELOW

QUOTE ONE®
Cost to build? See page 198 to order complete cost estimate to build this house in your area!

Design by
©**Home Planners**

Design
Q499

First Floor:
1,157 sq. ft.

Second Floor:
638 sq. ft.

Total:
1,795 sq. ft.

Width:
36'-0"

Depth:
40'-0"

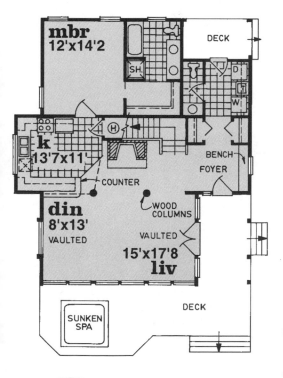

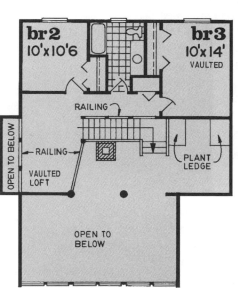

Design by
©Select Home Designs

This leisure home is perfect for outdoor living with French doors opening to a large sun deck and sunken spa. The open-beam, vaulted ceiling and high window wall provide views for the living and dining rooms, which are decorated with wood columns and warmed by a fireplace. The step-saving U-shaped kitchen has ample counter space and a bar counter to the dining room. The master bedroom on the first floor features a walk-in closet and bath with twin vanity, shower and soaking tub. A convenient mud room, with adjoining laundry, accesses a rear deck. Two bedrooms are on the second floor and share a full bath. Plans include details for both a basement and a crawlspace foundation.

Design Z054

First Floor:
576 sq. ft.

Second Floor:
480 sq. ft.

Total:
1,056 sq. ft.

Width:
24'-0"

Depth:
24'-0"

I f you have a site with beautiful lakeside views, this is the perfect plan for you! Windows abound, from the front-facing sun room to the wall of windows off the dining/living area where sliding doors open to an expansive veranda. An overhead pergola extends living outwards and provides shade for outdoor dining and relaxing. A rounded-hearth fireplace is a focal point of the living area. Two bedrooms are secluded upstairs and share a full bath. The master bedroom provides room for a private sitting area.

3,40 X 2,00
11'-4" X 6'-8"

3,30 X 2,70
11'-0" X 9'-0"

3,30 X 4,10
11'-0" X 13'-8"

3,30 X 1,60
11'-0" X 5'-4"

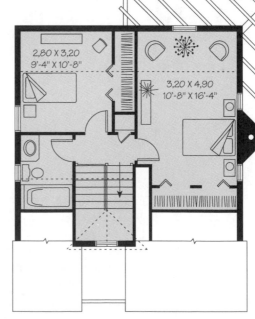

2,80 X 3,20
9'-4" X 10'-8"

3,20 X 4,90
10'-8" X 16'-4"

Design by

Design
Q202

Square Footage: 680

Bonus Room: 419 sq. ft.

Width: 26'-6"

Depth: 28'-0"

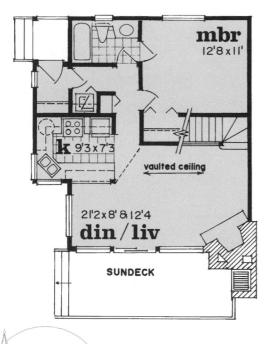

mbr
12'8 x 11'

k 9'3 x 7'3

vaulted ceiling

21'2 x 8' & 12'4
din / liv

SUNDECK

Design by
©Select Home Designs

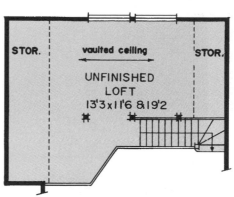

STOR.   vaulted ceiling   STOR.

UNFINISHED LOFT
13'3 x 11'6 & 19'2

Full window walls flood the living room and the dining room of this rustic lakeside home with natural light. A full sun deck with a built-in barbecue sits just outside the living area and is accessed by sliding glass doors. The entire large living space has a vaulted ceiling to gain spaciousness and to allow for the full height of the windows. The efficient U-shaped kitchen has a pass-through counter to the dining area and a window corner sink. A master bedroom on the first floor has the use of a full bath. A vaulted loft on the second floor overlooks the living room. It provides an additional 419 square feet not included in the above total. Use it for an additional bedroom or as a studio.

Design
Y045

First Floor:
862 sq. ft.

Second Floor:
332 sq. ft.

Total:
1,194 sq. ft.

Width:
42'-0"

Depth:
36'-2"

The front of this two-bedroom home is sweet and simple, while the rear is dedicated to fun and sun. Inside, the foyer opens to the two-story great room, where sunlight pours into the room not only from the wall of windows but also from four skylights. A large stone fireplace dominates the window wall and offers warmth on cool spring evenings.

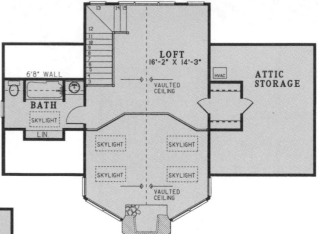

The L-shaped kitchen features French doors out to the grilling porch, perfect for numerous cookouts. On the opposite side of the home, a large master suite awaits to pamper the homeowner. Here, a second set of French doors leads out to the deck. Upstairs, a loft offers a walk-in closet and a full bath with a skylight.

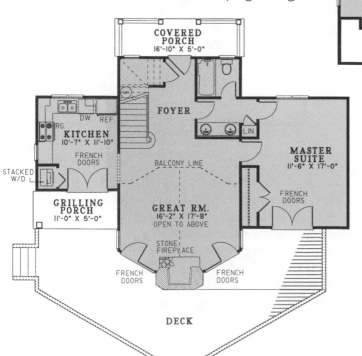

© Nelson Design Group, LLC

Design Z087

First Floor:
678 sq. ft.

Second Floor:
620 sq. ft.

Total:
1,298 sq. ft.

Width:
28'-0"

Depth:
40'-0"

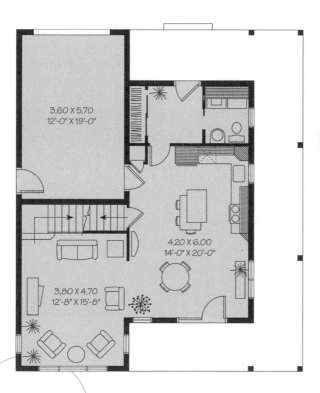

3,60 X 5,70
12'-0" X 19'-0"

4,20 X 6,00
14'-0" X 20'-0"

3,80 X 4,70
12'-8" X 15'-8"

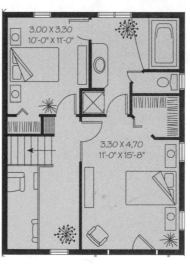

3,00 X 3,30
10'-0" X 11'-0"

3,30 X 4,70
11'-0" X 15'-8"

Large windows, a covered porch and an upper balcony make this home perfect for waterfront living. Inside, find a very comfortable plan including a family room, dining room with French-door access to the patio, and an L-shaped kitchen with breakfast area. A convenient powder room and laundry facilities are also on this floor. Upstairs are the two bedrooms that share a full bath with a separate tub and shower. The larger bedroom has French doors opening to the balcony.

Design by
©Drummond Designs, Inc.

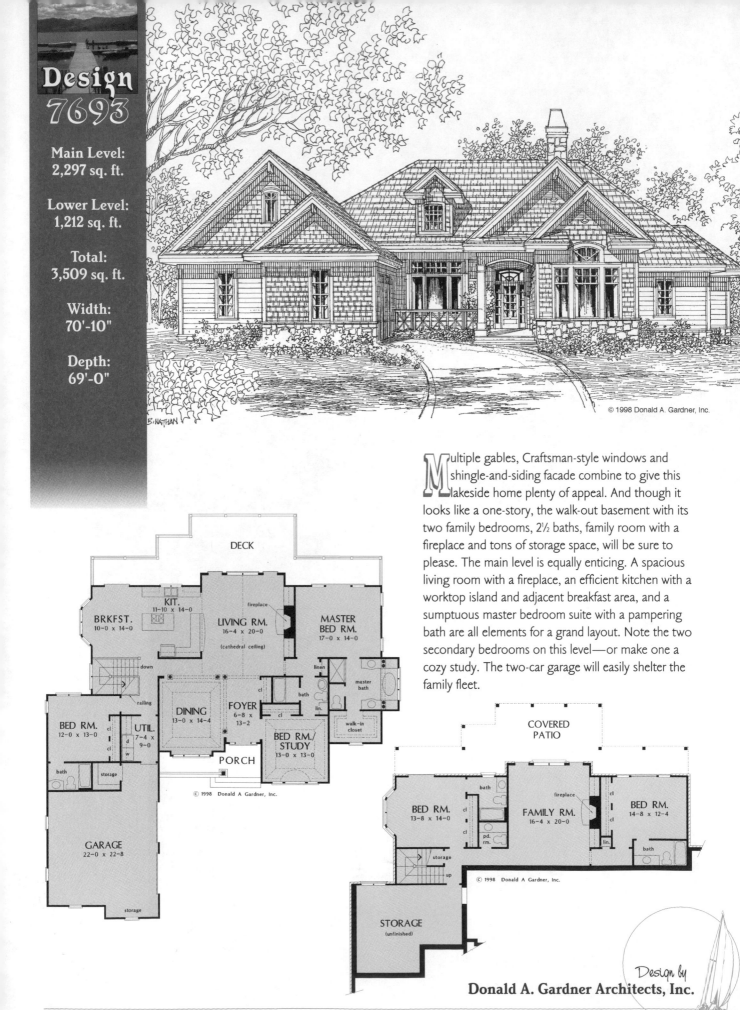

Design
7693

Main Level:
2,297 sq. ft.

Lower Level:
1,212 sq. ft.

Total:
3,509 sq. ft.

Width:
70'-10"

Depth:
69'-0"

© 1998 Donald A. Gardner, Inc.

Multiple gables, Craftsman-style windows and shingle-and-siding facade combine to give this lakeside home plenty of appeal. And though it looks like a one-story, the walk-out basement with its two family bedrooms, 2½ baths, family room with a fireplace and tons of storage space, will be sure to please. The main level is equally enticing. A spacious living room with a fireplace, an efficient kitchen with a worktop island and adjacent breakfast area, and a sumptuous master bedroom suite with a pampering bath are all elements for a grand layout. Note the two secondary bedrooms on this level—or make one a cozy study. The two-car garage will easily shelter the family fleet.

DECK

KIT.
11-10 x 14-0

BRKFST.
10-0 x 14-0

LIVING RM.
16-4 x 20-0
(cathedral ceiling)

fireplace

MASTER
BED RM.
17-0 x 14-0

linen

master
bath

down

railing

DINING
13-0 x 14-4

FOYER
6-8 x
13-2

cl

bath

lin.

walk-in
closet

BED RM.
12-0 x 13-0

UTIL.
7-4 x
9-0

cl

cl

d

w

bath

storage

BED RM./
STUDY
13-0 x 13-0

PORCH

GARAGE
22-0 x 22-8

storage

© 1998 Donald A Gardner, Inc.

COVERED
PATIO

bath

fireplace

cl

BED RM.
13-8 x 14-0

cl

cl

FAMILY RM.
16-4 x 20-0

pd.
rm.

lin.

cl

BED RM.
14-8 x 12-4

bath

storage

up

© 1998 Donald A Gardner, Inc.

STORAGE
(unfinished)

Design by
Donald A. Gardner Architects, Inc.

B. NATHAN

© 1998 Donald A. Gardner, Inc.

Design
7707

First Floor:
3,040 sq. ft.

Lower Floor:
1,736 sq. ft.

Total:
4,776 sq. ft.

Width:
106'-5"

Depth:
104'-2"

Looking a bit like a mountain resort, this fine Craftsman home is sure to be the envy of your neighborhood. Entering through the elegant front door, one finds an open staircase to the right and a spacious great room directly ahead. Here, a fireplace and a wall of windows give a cozy welcome. A lavish master suite begins with a sitting room complete with a fireplace, and continues to a private porch, large walk-in closet and sumptuous bedroom area. Two family bedrooms share a bath and have a wing to themselves. The efficient kitchen is adjacent to a large, sunny dining area, and offers access to a screened porch with yet another fireplace! The lower level consists of a huge media room with a fourth fireplace, two spacious bedrooms, each with private baths and tons of storage. A three-car garage, with extra space for storage, a golf cart or even a boat, will be perfect for the family fleet.

PORCH

media/rec. room below

railing

PORCH

MASTER
BED RM.
15-0 x 15-0
(cathedral ceiling)

fireplace

SCREEN
PORCH
14-10 x 15-6
(cathedral ceiling)

DINING
15-8 x 15-8
(cathedral ceiling)

GREAT RM.
21-8 x 21-0
(cathedral ceiling)

exposed beams

STUDY/
SITTING
12-4 x 16-0
fireplace

linen

master
bath

PORCH

wet bar

oven

railing

fireplace

walk-in
closet

built-in
cab.

pd.
rm.

down

KITCHEN
15-8 x 13-2

FOYER
21-8 x 5-6

sto.

cl

cl

BED RM.
12-0 x 14-0

LAUNDRY
10-6 x 12-2

cl

pan.

PORCH

walk-in
closet

cl

BED RM.
12-0 x 14-0

bath

© 1998 Donald A. Gardner, Inc.

GARAGE
23-7 x 35-7

STORAGE/
GOLF CART
11-4 x 8-0

COVERED
PATIO

balcony above

COVERED
PATIO

BED RM.
13-0 x 15-8

MEDIA/
REC. RM.
21-8 x 24-0

fireplace

BED RM.
22-3 x 15-10

cl

bath

bath

wet
bar

up

lin.

bath

walk-in
closet

STORAGE
(unfinished)

MECHANICAL
23-5 x 22-2

Design by
Donald A. Gardner Architects, Inc.

Design F154

First Floor:
836 sq. ft.

Second Floor:
481 sq. ft.

Total:
1,317 sq. ft.

Width:
38'-2"

Depth:
34'-0"

This sweet lakeside cottage is sure to please with its quaint charm and convenient floor plan. A covered porch greets family and friends and offers a place to sit and enjoy the summer breezes. Inside, the living room—with its warming fireplace—flows nicely into the kitchen/dining area. A snack bar, pantry and plenty of cabinet and counter space are just some of the features found here. The first-floor master suite has a bay window, walk-in closet and private bath. Upstairs, two bedrooms share a bath and a linen closet.

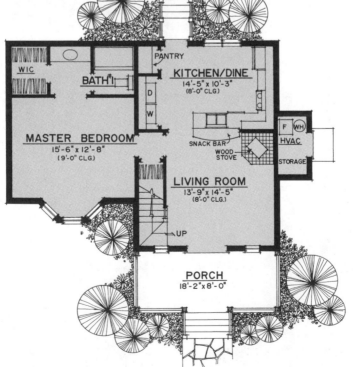

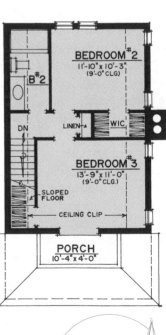

Design by
©R.L. Pfotenhauer

Design
F155

First Floor:
448 sq. ft.

Second Floor:
448 sq. ft.

Total:
896 sq. ft.

Width:
16'-0"

Depth:
41'-6"

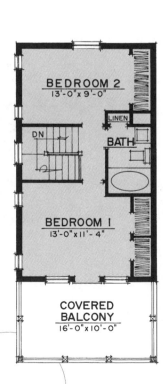

BEDROOM 2
13'-0" x 9'-0"

LINEN

DN

BATH

BEDROOM 1
13'-0" x 11'-4"

COVERED
BALCONY
16'-0" x 10'-0"

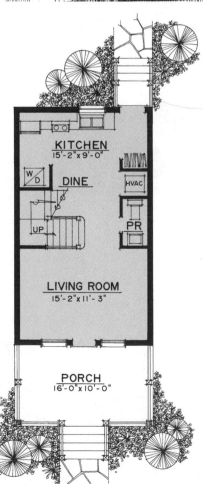

KITCHEN
15'-2" x 9'-0"

W/D

DINE

HVAC

UP

PR

LIVING ROOM
15'-2" x 11'-3"

PORCH
16'-0" x 10'-0"

Perfect for a lakeside vacation or starter home, this two-story design is sure to be a favorite. A large covered porch is available for watching sunrises over the water, while inside the living room is spacious and convenient to the kitchen and dining area. A powder room finishes off this level. Upstairs, the sleeping zone consists of two bedrooms and a full bath. Note how the front bedroom features its own covered balcony.

Design by
©R.L. Pfotenhauer

Design
Z098

First Floor:
1,092 sq. ft.

Second Floor:
996 sq. ft.

Total:
2,088 sq. ft.

Width:
38'-0"

Depth:
31'-4"

*This home, as shown in the photograph, may differ from the actual blueprints.
For more detailed information, please check the floor plans carefully.*

4,10 / 3,50 X 6,50
13'-8" / 11'-8" X 21'-8"

3,50 X 3,00
11'-8" X 10'-0"

3,50 X 3,60
11'-8" X 12'-0"

3,20 X 3,50
10'-8" X 11'-8"

5,30 X 4,10
17'-8" X 13'-8"

4,70 X 3,30
15'-8" X 11'-0"

4,70 X 4,60
15'-8" X 15'-4"

This delightful design has plenty to offer, and will surely be a family favorite. With a wraparound porch and a large rear deck, the indoor/outdoor relationships are perfect for entertaining. Inside, a living room opens to the right and features a fireplace and porch access. The kitchen and dining area are open to one another and encourage both formal and informal dinner parties. A sitting area at the back of the home is perfect for a quiet getaway. Upstairs, two family bedrooms and a large master bedroom—complete with a sitting area—share a lavish bath. This home is designed with a basement foundation.

Design by

©Drummond Designs, Inc.

Design
M529

First Floor:
2,780 sq. ft.

Second Floor:
878 sq. ft.

Total:
3,658 sq. ft.

Bonus Room:
206 sq. ft.

Width:
68'-3"

Depth:
89'-1"

The symmetrical front of this home conceals an imaginatively asymmetrical floor plan beyond. A keeping room, a sitting area in the master bedroom and a second bedroom all jut out from this home, forming interesting angles and providing extra window space for fine lakeside viewing. Two fireplaces, a gameroom, a study and His and Hers bathrooms in the master bedroom are interesting elements in this home. The bayed kitchen, with a walk-in pantry and a center island with room for seating, is sure to lure guests and family alike. The open floor plan and two-story ceilings in the family room add a modern touch.

Design by
©Andy McDonald Design Group

Design
9608

First Floor:
1,228 sq. ft.

Second Floor:
492 sq. ft.

Total:
1,720 sq. ft.

Width:
37'-6"

Depth:
46'-2"

An open and spacious interior with the best in up-to-date floor planning offers new excitement in this delightful country-style home. Besides the oversized great room with fireplace, there is a wonderful country kitchen with dining space. The sun room provides space for alternate dining and entertaining and a great place for watching sunsets over the water. The master suite is warmed by a fireplace and the adjacent sun room. Upstairs, there are two bedrooms, a full bath, a charming balcony and ample attic storage.

First Floor

seat

DECK
27-0 × 9-0

down
down
down

glass roof

SUN RM.
20-6 × 9-0

storage

wash
dry

KIT./DINING
14-2 × 9-0

pd. rm.

fireplace

MASTER BED RM.
13-0 × 16-8

balcony above

cl

cl

walk-in closet

GREAT RM.
16-0 × 18-0
fireplace

up

lin.   tub

master bath

PORCH
30-6 × 6-8

down

Second Floor

BED RM.
12-2 × 11-0

bath

cl
lin.

down

railing

great room below

attic storage

main roof

porch roof

BED RM.
11-0 × 14-10

cl   cl

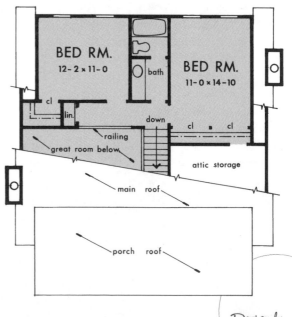

Design by

Donald A. Gardner Architects, Inc.

Design
4061
D

First Floor:
1,036 sq. ft.

Second Floor:
273 sq. ft.

Total:
1,309 sq. ft.

Width:
39'-0"

Depth:
38'-0"

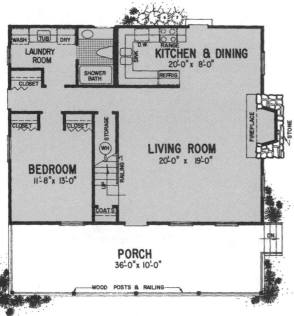

LAUNDRY ROOM

WASH | TUB | DRY

CLOSET

SHOWER BATH

KITCHEN & DINING
20'-0" x 8'-0"

D.W. | RANGE
SINK
REFRIG.

CLOSET | CLOSET

STORAGE

WH

FIREPLACE

STONE

BEDROOM
11'-8" x 13'-0"

LIVING ROOM
20'-0" x 19'-0"

UP

RAILING

COATS

DN

PORCH
36'-0" x 10'-0"

WOOD POSTS & RAILING

This charming farmhouse design will be economical to build and a pleasure to occupy. Like most vacation or waterfront homes, this design features an open plan. The large living area includes a living room, a dining room and a massive stone fireplace. A partition separates the kitchen from the living room. The first floor also holds a bedroom, a full bath and a laundry room. Upstairs is a spacious sleeping loft overlooking the living room. Don't miss the large front porch—this will be a favorite spot for relaxing.

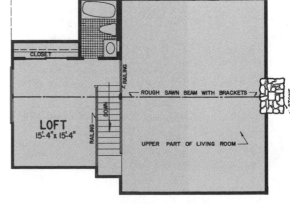

CLOSET

LOFT
15'-4" x 15'-4"

RAILING

DN

RAILING

ROUGH SAWN BEAM WITH BRACKETS

STONE

UPPER PART OF LIVING ROOM

QUOTE ONE®
Cost to build? See page 198
to order complete cost estimate
to build this house in your area!

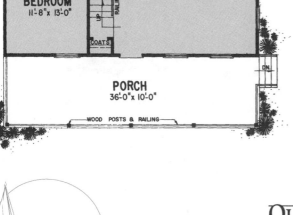

Design by
©**Home Planners**

129

Design N134

First Floor:
952 sq. ft.

Second Floor:
400 sq. ft.

Total:
1,352 sq. ft.

Width:
35'-10"

Depth:
32'-0"

Whether located in suburbia or on remote lakefront acreage, this leisure home is designed to bring optimum media entertainment into your life with a living room that doubles as a home entertainment center. The entertainment center is placed so that it is in full view of the living room, dining room and kitchen, which flow together in one large space. A bubble skylight floods the space with daylight. The dining space terminates with a solar bay and has access to the large rear deck, as does the living room. The entrance foyer leads to the main rooms as well as to the master bedroom off the bathroom hall. The bath features a double vanity. Also off the foyer is a well-lighted stairway to the second floor. Upstairs there are two bedrooms and a bath. Please specify basement, crawlspace or slab foundation when ordering.

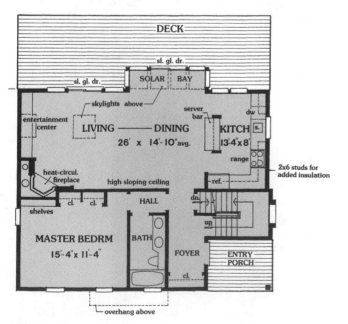

Design by

Design
4308

Main Level:
1,494 sq. ft.

Upper Level:
597 sq. ft.

Lower Level:
1,035 sq. ft.

Total:
3,126 sq. ft.

Width:
59'-0"

Depth:
69'-8"

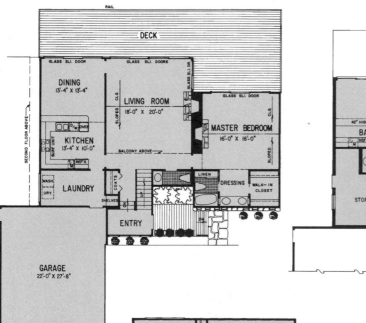

You can't help but feel spoiled by this design. Downstairs from the entry is a large living room with sloped ceiling and fireplace. Nearby is the U-shaped kitchen with a pass-through to the dining room. Also on this level, the master suite boasts a fireplace and a sliding glass door to the deck. The living and dining rooms also feature deck access. Upstairs are two bedrooms and a shared bath. A balcony sitting area overlooks the living room. Finish the lower level when your budget and space needs allow. It includes a play room with a fireplace, a half bath, a large bar and sliding glass doors to the patio.

Design by
©Home Planners

Design N132

First Floor:
1,100 sq. ft.

Second Floor:
519 sq. ft.

Total:
1,619 sq. ft.

Width:
48'-6"

Depth:
31'-4"

This home is a contemporary two-story salt box compactly designed within a total habitable area of 1,619 square feet. The rear facade is almost all glass, offering amazing waterfront views, and includes a greenhouse bay off the dining area. Properly oriented, the sun's rays will penetrate the glass wall and provide free heat in the winter. The living room and dining room merge into one huge space that appears to be larger than the dimensions because of the window area and the high sloped ceiling. There are turn-around stairs to the second floor, with a middle landing well-lit by a tall vertical window. The spacious bathrooms on both floors are so arranged that outside windows provide both ventilation and natural light. Finally, the exterior expresses what goes on inside. In the front, a conservative contemporary facade is enhanced by the second-floor overhang, which allows the second floor bedrooms to be enlarged. Please specify basement, crawlspace or slab foundation when ordering.

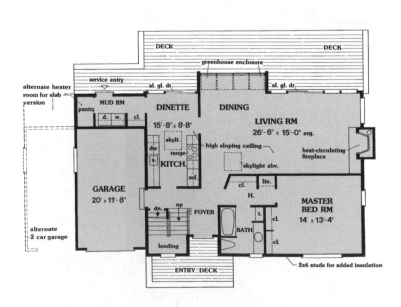

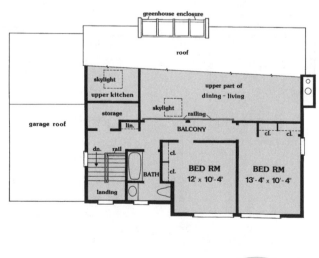

Design 9609

Square Footage: 1,426

Width: 67'-6"

Depth: 47'-8"

DECK
29-8 x 9-0

hot tub

down

skylights

SCREENED PORCH
29-0 x 10-0

clerestory above

BED RM.
10-8 x 11-0

ltn.

cl

bath

BED RM.
10-8 x 11-0

cl

fireplace

KIT.
8-10 x 11-8

MASTER BED RM.
13-4 x 17-0

walk in closet

GREAT RM.
20-0 x 21-6
(cathedral ceiling)

cl

pd. rm.

master bath

tub

FOYER

dry wash

PORCH
27-6 x 6-0

down

Rustic charm abounds in this amenity-filled three-bedroom plan. From the central living area, with cathedral ceiling and fireplace, to the sumptuous master suite, there are few features omitted. Be sure to notice the large walk-in closet in the master bedroom, the pampering whirlpool tub, and the separate water-closet compartment. Two other bedrooms have a connecting bath with a single-bowl vanity for each. The house wraps around a screened porch with skylights—a grand place for eating and entertaining. The spacious rear deck has plenty of room for a hot tub.

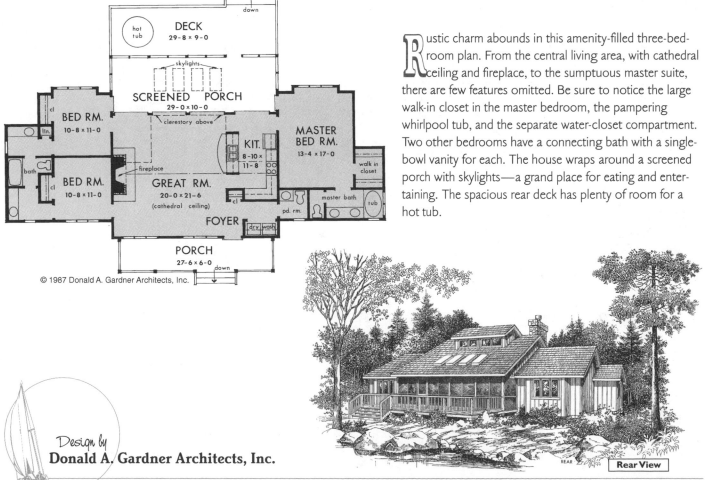

REAR

Rear View

Design by
Donald A. Gardner Architects, Inc.

Design
Q283

Square Footage:
1,679

Width:
58'-8"

Depth:
31'-10"

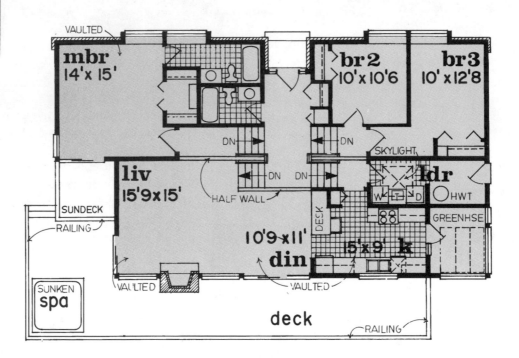

VAULTED

mbr
14'x 15'

br2
10'x 10'6

br3
10'x 12'8

SKYLIGHT

liv
15'9x15'

DN

DN

DN

DN

ldr

HALF WALL

W H D

HWT

SUNDECK

RAILING

DECK

88

GREENHSE

10'9x11'
din

15'x 9' **k**

SUNKEN
spa

VAULTED

VAULTED

deck

RAILING

With vertical wood siding and a large stone fireplace, this country retreat is the image of a rustic lakeside hideaway. A recessed entry opens to a central hall with bedrooms flanking it. A few steps down, the living areas are positioned to take advantage of outdoor views and the long deck with sunken spa that wraps two sides of the design. The living room, dining room and kitchen are all vaulted. The living room is further enhanced by a fireplace. A greenhouse just beyond the kitchen can serve as a breakfast room, if desired. Two family bedrooms share the use of a skylit bath and also have box-bay windows. The master suite has double box-bay windows, a walk-in closet, vaulted ceiling and a private sun deck. Clerestory windows illuminate the main entry and hallway.

Design by
©Select Home Designs

Design
N152

Square
Footage:
1,042

Width:
57'-8"

Depth:
36'-4"

This is a good-looking and viable waterfront house, ideal for the modest-income family. The large living/dining room features a ceiling that soars dramatically to just over thirteen feet near the window wall, two sets of sliding glass doors giving access to the outdoor deck and a fireplace covered with decorative stone. The efficient L-shaped kitchen also has direct access to the deck, making service convenient and waterfront views available. Note the storage/utility area off the deck. A hall leads off to the right to a bedroom and bath and then farther to the master bedroom and a second family bedroom. The carport could either shelter your car or the family boat.

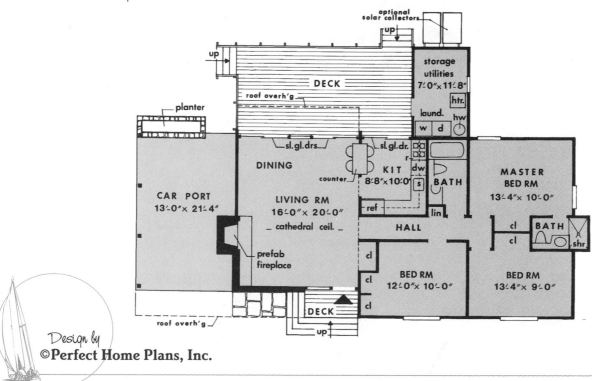

Design by
©Perfect Home Plans, Inc.

Design
7632

Square Footage:
1,680

Width:
62'-8"

Depth:
59'-10"

©1997 Donald A. Gardner Architects, Inc.

DECK

fireplace
(cathedral ceiling)

SCREEN PORCH
17-4 x 13-8

(cathedral ceiling)

DINING
10-10 x 13-0

GREAT RM.
16-10 x 17-8

BED RM.
11-0 x 11-0

cl

cl

lin

bath

(cathedral ceiling)

KIT.
11-4 x 15-0

fireplace

cl

MASTER BED RM.
14-4 x 15-0

walk-in closet

FOYER
9-9 x 5-8

BED RM.
11-0 x 11-0

cl

master bath

w d
UTIL
8-0 x 5-4

PORCH

lin

© 1997 Donald A. Gardner Architects, Inc.

Rear View

GARAGE
22-0 x 22-0

This rustic retreat is updated with contemporary angles and packs a lot of living into a small space. Indoor/outdoor relationships are well developed and help to create a comfortable home. Start off with the covered front porch, which leads to a welcoming foyer. The beam-ceilinged great room opens directly ahead and features a fireplace, a wall of windows, access to the screened porch (with its own fireplace!) and is adjacent to the angled dining area. A highly efficient island kitchen is sure to please with a cathedral ceiling, access to the rear deck and tons of counter and cabinet space. Two family bedrooms, sharing a full bath, are located on one end of the plan, while the master suite is secluded for complete privacy at the other end. The master suite includes a walk-in closet and a pampering bath.

Design by
Donald A. Gardner Architects, Inc.

© 1987 Donald A. Gardner Architects, Inc.

Design
9607

Square
Footage:
1,299

Width:
65'-4"

Depth:
44'-0"

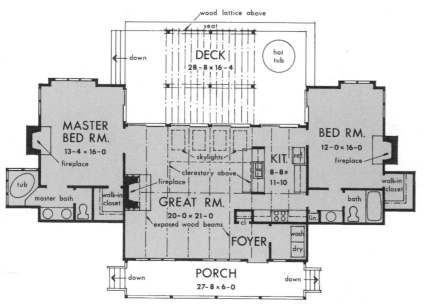

wood lattice above

seat

DECK
28-8 × 16-4

hot tub

← down

**MASTER
BED RM.**
13-4 × 16-0
fireplace

skylights

clerestory above

fireplace

tub

master bath

walk-in closet

GREAT RM.
20-0 × 21-0
exposed wood beams

KIT.
8-8 ×
11-10

ref.

BED RM.
12-0 × 16-0
fireplace

walk-in closet

bath

cl

lin.

FOYER

wash

dry

← down

PORCH
27-8 × 6-0

down →

© 1987 Donald A. Gardner Architects, Inc.

Though rustic in appearance, this two-bedroom plan provides all the features sought after in today's well-planned waterfront home. A large central area includes a great room, entrance foyer and kitchen with serving and eating counter. Note the use of cathedral ceilings with exposed wood beams, skylights, clerestory windows and a fireplace in this area. The master suite has an optional fireplace, a walk-in closet and a whirlpool tub. The second bedroom also has an optional fireplace and a full bath. All rooms open to the rear deck—perfect for those lakeside views—which supplies space for a hot tub.

Rear View

Design by
Donald A. Gardner Architects, Inc.

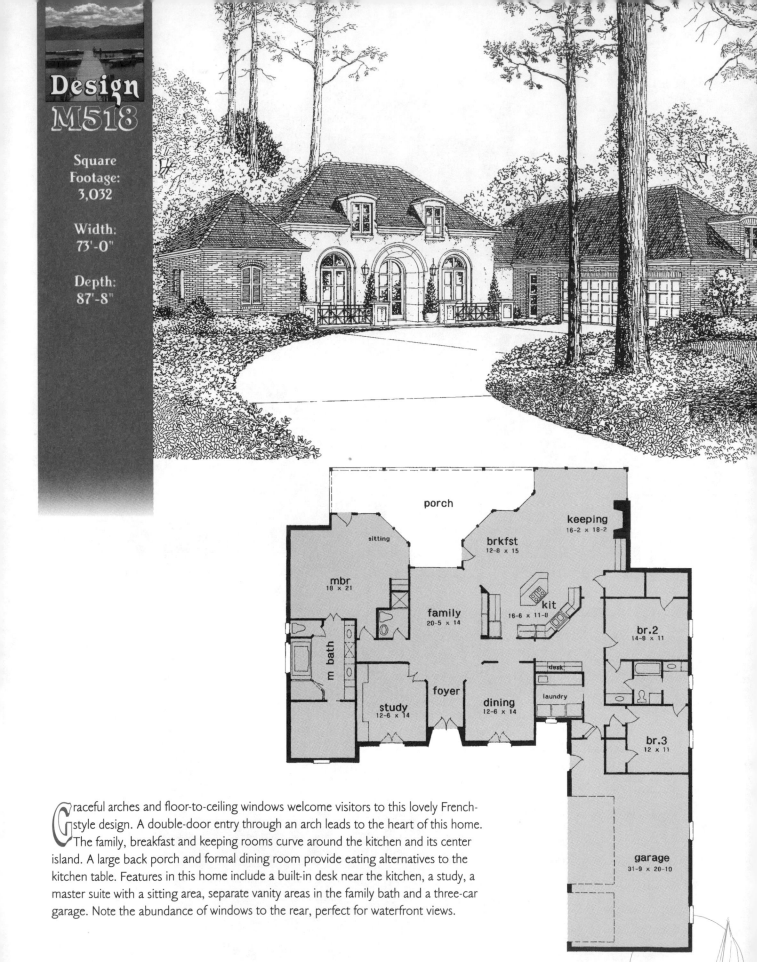

Design
M518

Square Footage:
3,032

Width:
73'-0"

Depth:
87'-8"

porch

keeping
16-2 x 18-2

sitting

brkfst
12-8 x 15

mbr
18 x 21

kit
16-6 x 11-8

family
20-5 x 14

br.2
14-8 x 11

m bath

desk

study
12-6 x 14

foyer

dining
12-6 x 14

laundry

br.3
12 x 11

garage
31-9 x 20-10

Graceful arches and floor-to-ceiling windows welcome visitors to this lovely French-style design. A double-door entry through an arch leads to the heart of this home. The family, breakfast and keeping rooms curve around the kitchen and its center island. A large back porch and formal dining room provide eating alternatives to the kitchen table. Features in this home include a built-in desk near the kitchen, a study, a master suite with a sitting area, separate vanity areas in the family bath and a three-car garage. Note the abundance of windows to the rear, perfect for waterfront views.

Design by

This classic French country home is certainly appealing from the front, but the rear holds a surprise—it's virtually walled with windows! The foyer is flanked by a study and the formal dining room, and opens to the light and spacious family room with a fireplace and wet bar. To the right, the large kitchen opens to a breakfast area, which has elegant double-door access to the covered porch.

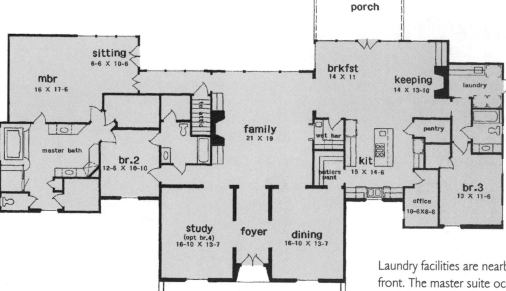

Laundry facilities are nearby, and an office is tucked away up front. The master suite occupies the left side of the plan with a huge, compartmented master bath and windowed sitting area. Two additional bedrooms, each close to a full bath, keep family and friends comfortable.

Design by
©Andy McDonald Design Group

Design
Z264

First Floor:
1,024 sq. ft.

Second Floor:
456 sq. ft.

Total:
1,480 sq. ft.

Width:
32'-0"

Depth:
40'-0"

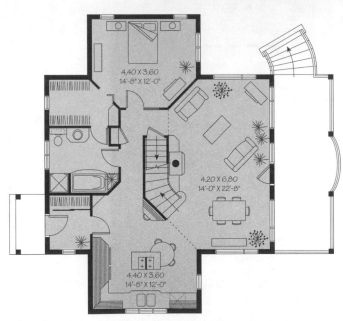

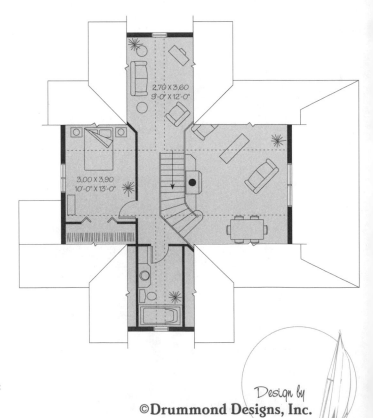

A daylight basement provides a walk-out to ground level on this charming waterfront cottage. Inside, the family and dining rooms combine for a feeling of spaciousness, a feeling heightened by access to a large covered porch. The L-shaped kitchen has an island with seating for quick or casual meals. The downstairs bedroom has a huge walk-in closet and access to a full bath. Upstairs is another full bath, a sitting area and a room that could be used as a study or another bedroom.

© Drummond Designs, Inc.

Design
Q201

Square Footage: 936

Bonus Loft: 358 sq. ft.

Width: 30'-0"

Depth: 32'-0"

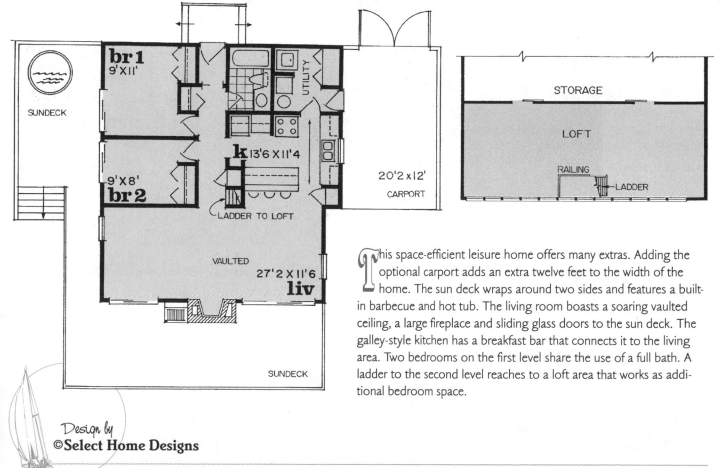

SUNDECK

br 1 9'X11'

br 2 9'X8'

UTILITY

k 13'6 X 11'4

LADDER TO LOFT

VAULTED

27'2 X 11'6 **liv**

20'2 x12' CARPORT

SUNDECK

STORAGE

LOFT

RAILING

LADDER

This space-efficient leisure home offers many extras. Adding the optional carport adds an extra twelve feet to the width of the home. The sun deck wraps around two sides and features a built-in barbecue and hot tub. The living room boasts a soaring vaulted ceiling, a large fireplace and sliding glass doors to the sun deck. The galley-style kitchen has a breakfast bar that connects it to the living area. Two bedrooms on the first level share the use of a full bath. A ladder to the second level reaches to a loft area that works as additional bedroom space.

Design by
©**Select Home Designs**

Design
Q206

Square Footage:
988

Width:
38'-0"

Depth:
26'-0"

This cozy design serves nicely as a leisure home for vacations, or as a full-time lakeside retirement residence. Horizontal siding and a solid-stone chimney stack are a reminder of a rustic retreat. A spacious living/dining area has a full wall of glass overlooking a deck with views beyond. A masonry fireplace warms the space in the cold months. A nearby U-shaped kitchen has a pass-through counter to the dining room. A large laundry/mud room across the hall holds storage space. Sleeping quarters are comprised of a large master suite and a smaller family bedroom, both with hall closets. A full bath serves both bedrooms.

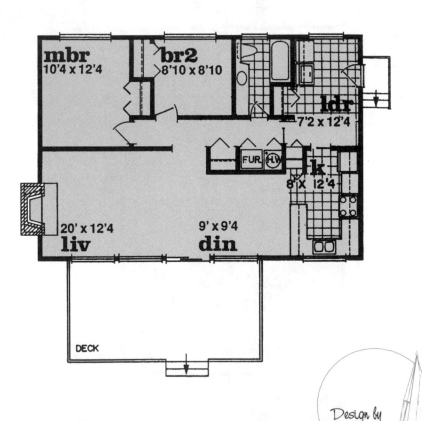

mbr
10'4 x 12'4

br2
8'10 x 8'10

ldr
7'2 x 12'4

FUR HW

k
8' x 12'4

liv
20' x 12'4

din
9' x 9'4

DECK

Design Q325

First Floor:
1,186 sq. ft.

Second Floor:
597 sq. ft.

Total:
1,783 sq. ft.

Width:
39'-4"

Depth:
41'-4"

A partially covered, wraparound deck on this waterfront home allows for outdoor relaxation; a sunken spa adds to the enjoyment. The central fireplace between the vaulted living room and dining room warms both areas. A breakfast counter separates the kitchen from the dining room.

The luxurious master suite sits to the rear of the first floor with a bath that contains a whirlpool tub. A half bath is located near the entry, adjacent to a laundry/storage area. The second floor holds a full bath and two additional bedrooms—one with a built-in desk.

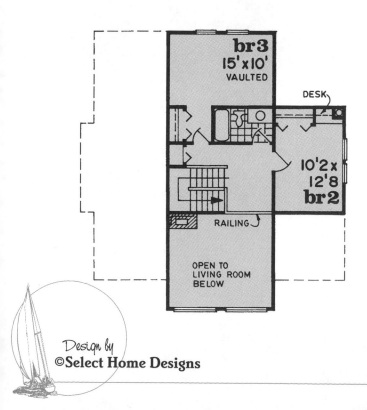

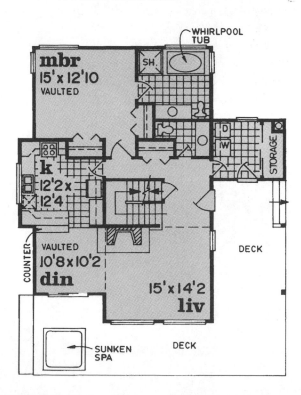

Design by
©Select Home Designs

Design
HPT7230005

First Floor:
605 sq. ft.

Second Floor:
432 sq. ft.

Total:
1,037 sq. ft.

Width:
33'-9"

Depth:
27'-6"

A shed-dormered roof with rolled eaves, a great stone chimney and a shingled exterior lend rusticity to this Craftsman-inspired retreat. Multi-wooden posts are anchored by stone piers, framing the welcoming front entry. Inside, a stone fireplace warms the living room, providing an ideal setting to curl up with a good book and enjoy the window seat that graces the bay window overlooking the front yard. A countertop separates the kitchen from the dining area, where sliding glass doors lead to a rear patio. The second floor contains two bedrooms and a full bath, one of which features a trio of period-style windows set into a centered dormer.

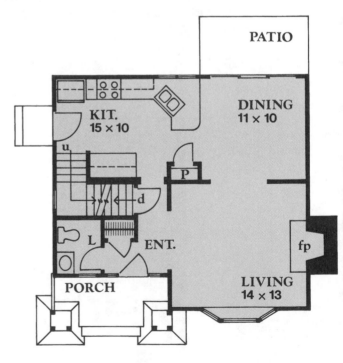

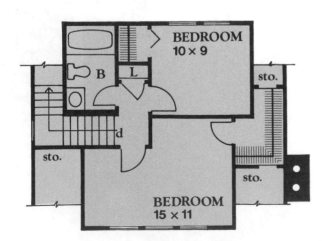

Design by
©R. L. Pfotenhauer

Design
HPT7230006

Square Footage:
1,404

Width:
54'-7"

Depth:
46'-6"

This rustic Craftsman-style cottage is perfect for the riverside and provides an open interior with good outdoor flow. The front covered porch invites casual gatherings, while inside, the dining area is set for both everyday and planned occasions. Meal preparations are a breeze with a cooktop/snack-bar island in the kitchen. A centered fireplace in the great room shares its warmth with the dining room. A rear hall leads to the master bedroom and a secondary bedroom upstairs. The loft has space for computers.

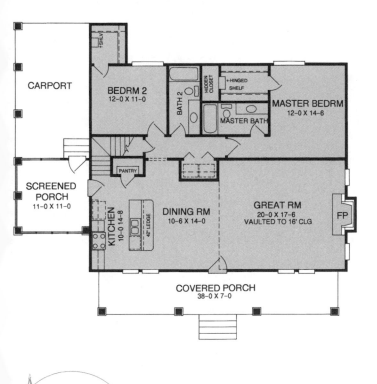

CARPORT

BEDRM 2
12-0 X 11-0

BATH 2

HIDDEN CLOSET

←HINGED SHELF

MASTER BEDRM
12-0 X 14-6

MASTER BATH

PANTRY

SCREENED PORCH
11-0 X 11-0

KITCHEN
10-0 14-8

42" LEDGE

DINING RM
10-6 X 14-0

GREAT RM
20-0 X 17-6
VAULTED TO 16' CLG

FP

COVERED PORCH
38-0 X 7-0

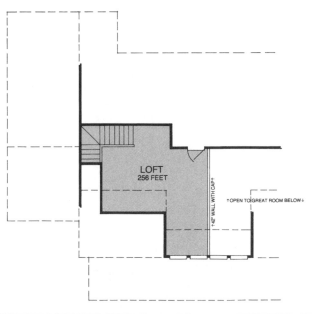

LOFT
256 FEET

↑42" WALL WITH CAP↑

↑OPEN TO GREAT ROOM BELOW↓

Design by
©Larry E. Belk Designs

Design
HPT7230007

First Floor:
1,431 sq. ft.

Second Floor:
1,054 sq. ft.

Total:
2,485 sq. ft.

Width:
40'-0"

Depth:
60'-0"

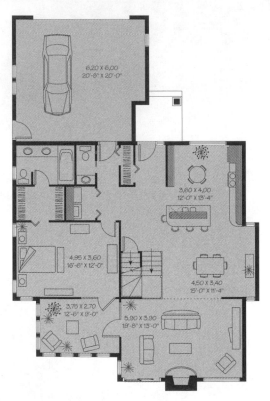

Whether your views are mountain, water, woodland or desert, this contemporary home allows you to incorporate them into your decor through its large windows. The main-level master suite privately accesses a sun room. For those who want a direct dose of the elements, there is a large open deck. The main living area is open, so that a fireplace in the living room can be seen from the dining room and kitchen. Three bedrooms, two bathrooms and a powder room complete the plan. This home is designed with a basement foundation.

UP ON STILTS

Designs with pier foundations

Design 6654 by The Sater Design Collection. See page 150 for details

Design E203

First Floor:
1,056 sq. ft.

Second Floor:
807 sq. ft.

Total:
1,863 sq. ft.

Width:
33'-0"

Depth:
37'-0"

Run up a flight of stairs to an attractive four-bedroom home! With a traditional flavor, this fine pier design is sure to please. Indoor/outdoor relationships are abundant, ranging from the front deck/porch to the private master balcony, as well as the small deck and rear stairs off the dining area. The great room features a fireplace and easy access to the L-shaped kitchen.

Here, a work top island makes meal preparation a breeze. Two family bedrooms share a full bath and access to the laundry facilities. Upstairs, a third bedroom offers a private bath and two walk-in closets. The master suite is complete with a pampering bath, two walk-in closets and a large private balcony.

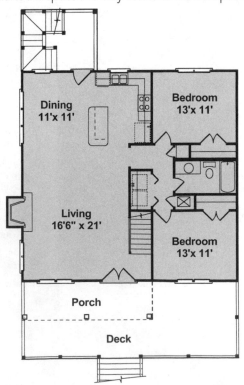

Dining
11' x 11'

Bedroom
13' x 11'

Living
16'6" x 21'

Bedroom
13' x 11'

Porch

Deck

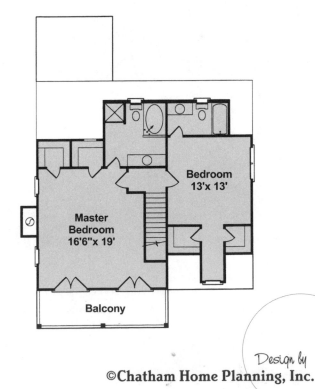

Master
Bedroom
16'6" x 19'

Bedroom
13' x 13'

Balcony

Design by

©Chatham Home Planning, Inc.

148

Design
Z117

First Floor:
962 sq. ft.

Second Floor:
1,076 sq. ft.

Third Floor:
342 sq. ft.

Total:
2,380 sq. ft.

Width:
39'-8"

Depth:
36'-8"

This luxurious pier home, with interesting window details and outdoor staircases, will be a popular spot on the beach. Guests will always be welcome with three bedrooms on the first floor and another on the third. A private master suite on the second floor keeps the owners comfortable too. There are two family rooms, one with a fireplace, a formal dining room and an efficient kitchen with a breakfast bar. A laundry room and 3½ bathrooms keep everyone clean.

Design by
©Drummond Designs, Inc.

Design 6654

First Floor:
1,342 sq. ft.

Second Floor:
511 sq. ft.

Total:
1,853 sq. ft.

Width:
44'-0"

Depth:
40'-0"

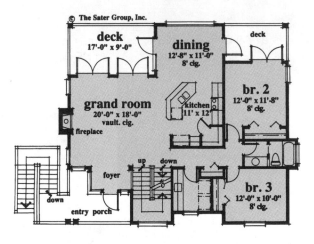

© The Sater Group, Inc.

deck 17'-0" x 9'-0"

dining 12'-8" x 11'-0" 8' clg.

deck

grand room 20'-0" x 18'-0" vault. clg.

kitchen 11' x 12

br. 2 12'-0" x 11'-8" 8' clg.

fireplace

up   down

foyer

down

entry porch

br. 3 12'-0" x 10'-0" 8' clg.

With influences from homes of the Caribbean, this island home is a perfect seaside residence or primary residence. The main living area is comprised of a grand room with a fireplace and access to a deck. The dining space also accesses this deck plus another that it shares with a secondary bedroom. An L-shaped kitchen with a prep island is open to the living areas. Two bedrooms on this level share a full bath. The master suite dominates the upper level. It has an observation deck and a bath with dual vanities and a whirlpool tub.

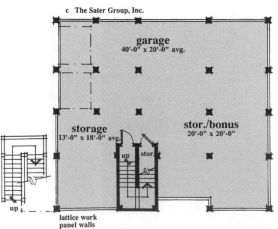

c The Sater Group, Inc.

garage 40'-0" x 20'-0" avg.

storage 13'-0" x 18'-0" avg.

stor./bonus 20'-0" x 20'-0"

up   stor.

up

lattice work panel walls

observation deck

master 13'-0" x 14'-0" vault. clg.

am kitchen

open to grand room below

down

© The Sater Group, Inc.

Design 8744

First Floor:
1,073 sq. ft.

Second Floor:
470 sq. ft.

Total:
1,543 sq. ft.

Width:
30'-0"

Depth:
71'-6"

J.N. HANSEN S.D.G.

Holding the narrowest of footprints, this adorable little plan is big on interior space—perfect for low-lying beachfront areas. The family room has three big windows and opens to the tiled, U-shaped kitchen and breakfast nook, with access to the rear deck. The master bedroom, which includes a walk-in closet, and another bedroom share a full bath on this floor. Two more bedrooms and another full bath are upstairs. Bedroom 4 features a study area in the dormer.

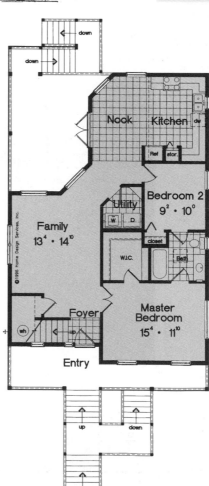

Design by
©Home Design Services, Inc.

Design
HPT7230008

First Floor:
2,146 sq. ft.

Second Floor:
952 sq. ft.

Vestibule:
187 sq. ft.

Total:
3,285 sq. ft.

Width:
52'-0"

Depth:
65'-4"

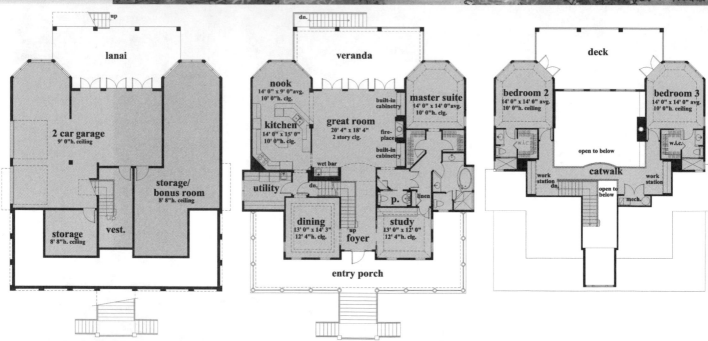

lanai

up

2 car garage
9' 0"h. ceiling

storage/
bonus room
8' 8"h. ceiling

storage
8' 8"h. ceiling

vest.

---

dn.

veranda

nook
14' 0" x 9' 0" avg.
10' 0"h. clg.

kitchen
14' 0" x 15' 0"
10' 0"h. clg.

great room
20' 4" x 18' 4"
2 story clg.

built-in
cabinetry

fire-
place

built-in
cabinetry

master suite
14' 0" x 14' 0" avg.
10' 0"h. clg.

wet bar

utility

dn.

p.

linen

dining
13' 0" x 14' 3"
12' 4"h. clg.

up

foyer

study
13' 0" x 12' 0"
12' 4"h. clg.

entry porch

---

deck

bedroom 2
14' 0" x 14' 0" avg.
10' 0" ceiling

bedroom 3
14' 0" x 14' 0" avg.
10' 0" ceiling

w.i.c.

w.i.c.

open to below

work
station

catwalk

work
station

dn.

open to
below

mech.

An inviting wraparound porch and plenty of other outdoor spaces extend the living area of this great cottage. Built-in cabinetry, a massive fireplace and a host of French doors highlight the central living space, which also features a wet bar. Nearby, the morning nook provides a bay window and an interior vista that includes the central fireplace. A gourmet kitchen with a food-preparation island serves the formal dining room. The secluded master wing enjoys a bumped-out window, a stunning tray ceiling and twin walk-in closets. The upper level boasts a catwalk that over-looks the great room and the foyer, and connects the two secondary suites. Bedrooms 2 and 3 have walk-in closets, spacious baths and individual access to the upper deck.

Design by

©The Sater Design Collection

© 1998 Donald A. Gardner Architects, Inc.

Design 7738

First Floor:
1,366 sq. ft.

Second Floor:
689 sq. ft.

Total:
2,055 sq. ft.

Width:
49'-8"

Depth:
50'-6"

B. NATHAN

BALCONY
12-4 x 6-4

MASTER BED RM.
12-4 x 16-4

skylights

fireplace

(cathedral ceiling)

attic storage

walk-in closet

master bath

handrail

down

LOFT/STUDY
10-1 x 11-4
(cathedral ceiling)

shelves

palladian window

down

PORCH

fireplace

GREAT RM.
14-0 x 16-0

BED RM.
12-0 x 11-0

bath

KIT.
12-0 x 11-0

pan.

DINING
12-8 x 11-0

walk-in closet

lin.

cl

UTIL.
6-0 x 8-0

w

d

up

down

FOYER
9-2 x 6-8

cl

BED RM.
12-0 x 11-0
(cathedral ceiling)

cl

down

PORCH

down

© 1998 Donald A. Gardner Architects, Inc.

With an elevated pier foundation, this stunning home is perfect for waterfront properties. Magnificent porches, a balcony and a plethora of picture windows take advantage of the beach or lakeside views. The great room features a ten-foot high beamed ceiling, a fireplace and a space saving built-in entertainment center. The staircase is highlighted by a grand window with an arched top, while a palladian window accents the upstairs loft/study. The master suite is the essence of luxury with skylights, a fireplace, cathedral ceiling, balcony, a spacious, vaulted bath, and an oversized walk-in closet.

Design by
Donald A. Gardner Architects, Inc.

Design
6618

Main Level:
1,944 sq. ft.

Upper Level:
1,196 sq. ft.

Total:
3,140 sq. ft.

Lower Level:
195 sq. ft.

Width:
68'-0"

Depth:
54'-0"

In the deluxe grand room of this Floridian home, family and friends will enjoy the ambience created by arches and access to a veranda. Two guest rooms flank a full bath—one of the guest rooms also sports a private deck. The kitchen serves a circular breakfast nook. Upstairs, a balcony overlook furthers the drama of the grand room. The master suite, with a deck and a private bath opening through a pocket door, will be a pleasure to occupy. Another bedroom—or use this room for a study—sits at the other side of this floor. It features a curved bay window, an expansive deck, built-ins and a full bath. The lower level contains enough room for two cars in its carport and offers plenty of storage and bonus room.

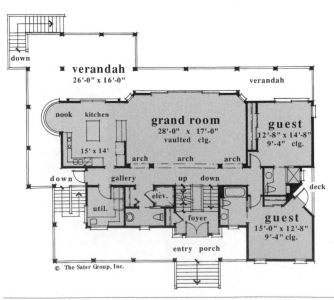

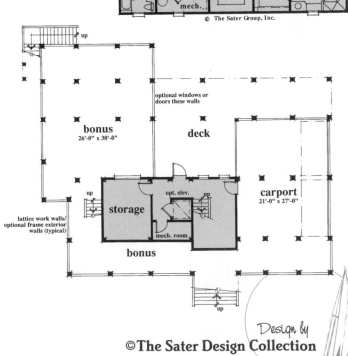

Design by
©The Sater Design Collection

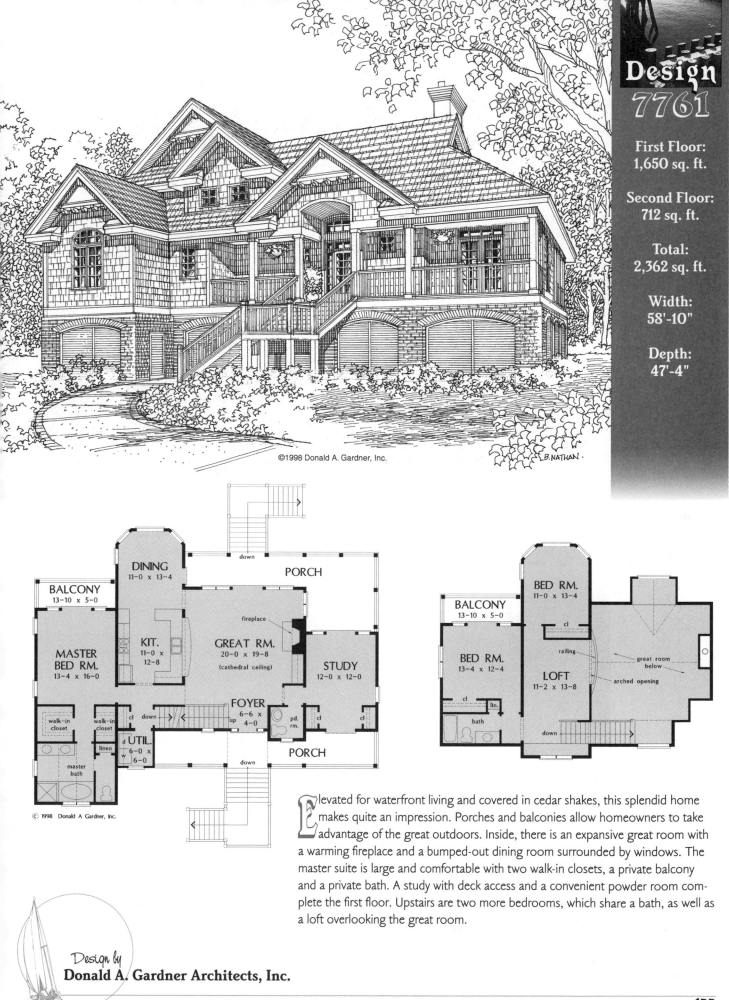

Design 7761

First Floor:
1,650 sq. ft.

Second Floor:
712 sq. ft.

Total:
2,362 sq. ft.

Width:
58'-10"

Depth:
47'-4"

©1998 Donald A. Gardner, Inc.

L.B. NATHAN

© 1998 Donald A Gardner, Inc.

BALCONY
13-10 x 5-0

DINING
11-0 x 13-4

PORCH

KIT.
11-0 x 12-8

GREAT RM.
20-0 x 19-8
(cathedral ceiling)

fireplace

MASTER BED RM.
13-4 x 16-0

STUDY
12-0 x 12-0

walk-in closet

walk-in closet

cl

down

FOYER
6-6 x 4-0

up

pd. rm.

cl

cl

linen

UTIL.
6-0 x 6-0

d

w

master bath

down

PORCH

down

BALCONY
13-10 x 5-0

BED RM.
11-0 x 13-4

cl

BED RM.
13-4 x 12-4

railing

great room below

LOFT
11-2 x 13-8

arched opening

cl

lin.

bath

down

Elevated for waterfront living and covered in cedar shakes, this splendid home makes quite an impression. Porches and balconies allow homeowners to take advantage of the great outdoors. Inside, there is an expansive great room with a warming fireplace and a bumped-out dining room surrounded by windows. The master suite is large and comfortable with two walk-in closets, a private balcony and a private bath. A study with deck access and a convenient powder room complete the first floor. Upstairs are two more bedrooms, which share a bath, as well as a loft overlooking the great room.

Design by
Donald A. Gardner Architects, Inc.

Design
6616

First Floor:
1,136 sq. ft.

Second Floor:
636 sq. ft.

Total:
1,772 sq. ft.

Width:
41'-9"

Depth:
45'-0"

This two-story home's pleasing exterior is complemented by its warm character and decorative "widow's walk." The covered entry—with its dramatic transom window—leads to a spacious great room highlighted by a warming fireplace. To the right, the dining room and kitchen combine to provide a delightful place for mealtimes inside or out, with access to a side deck through double doors. Two bedrooms and a full bath complete the first floor. The luxurious master suite, located on the second floor for privacy, features an oversized walk-in closet and a separate dressing area. The pampering master bath enjoys a relaxing whirlpool tub, a double-bowl vanity and a compartmented toilet.

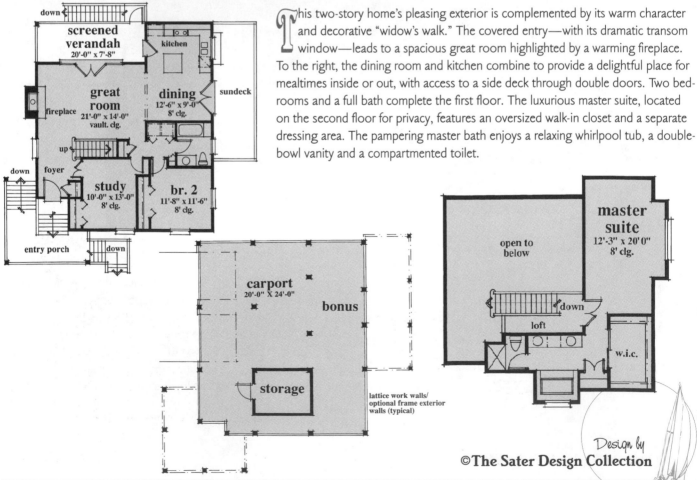

down

screened verandah
20'-0" x 7'-8"

kitchen

great room
21'-0" x 14'-0"
vault. clg.

dining
12'-6" x 9'-0"
8' clg.

sundeck

fireplace

up

down

foyer

study
10'-0" x 13'-0"
8' clg.

br. 2
11'-8" x 11'-6"
8' clg.

entry porch

down

carport
20'-0" X 24'-0"

bonus

storage

lattice work walls/
optional frame exterior
walls (typical)

open to below

master suite
12'-3" x 20'0"
8' clg.

down

loft

w.i.c.

Design 8751

First Floor:
1,125 sq. ft.

Second Floor:
554 sq. ft.

Total:
1,679 sq. ft.

Width:
33'-9"

Depth:
45'-0"

J.N. HANSEN P.T.L.

Ample windows and a large covered deck take advantage of the views from this coastal home. The foyer welcomes you to a versatile design, with a den or guest room to the left. A staircase leads to the private master bedroom suite, which has a spiral stair to the lookout high atop the roof. Back on the first floor, the large living room leads to an archway for the dining room. The island kitchen has access to the deck for summer lunches. The two secondary bedrooms are versatile and spacious.

Design
R152

First Floor:
944 sq. ft.

Second Floor:
826 sq. ft.

Total:
1,770 sq. ft.

Width:
30'-4"

Depth:
42'-8"

©1998 Donald A. Gardner, Inc.

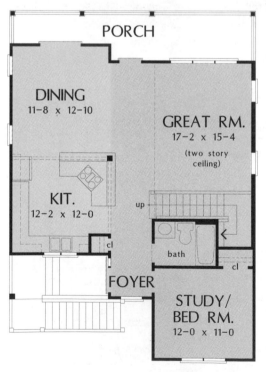

PORCH

DINING
11-8 x 12-10

GREAT RM.
17-2 x 15-4
(two story ceiling)

up

KIT.
12-2 x 12-0

cl

bath

cl

FOYER

STUDY/ BED RM.
12-0 x 11-0

© 1998   Donald A Gardner, Inc.

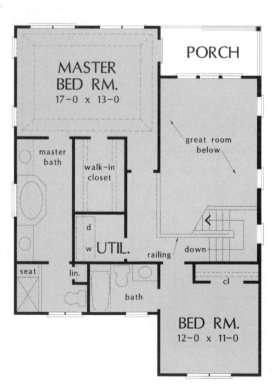

MASTER BED RM.
17-0 x 13-0

PORCH

master bath

walk-in closet

great room below

d

UTIL.

w

railing

down

seat

lin.

bath

cl

BED RM.
12-0 x 11-0

A coastal home, this plan features a super-slim design for very narrow lots. First- and second-floor porches maximize waterfront views. Windows in both the two-story great room and the dining room also emphasize the views. A large kitchen serves everyone easily and offers plenty of counter and cabinet space. A powder room and a study or extra bedroom complete the first floor. The master suite, with private bath and huge walk-in closet, is upstairs as is another bedroom and full bath.

Design by

Donald A. Gardner Architects, Inc.

Design
E161

First Floor:
912 sq. ft.

Second Floor:
831 sq. ft.

Total:
1,743 sq. ft.

Width:
34'-0"

Depth:
32'-0"

With a pier foundation, this two-story home is perfect for an oceanfront lot. The main level consists of an open living area that flows into the dining area adjacent to the kitchen. Here, a walk-in pantry and plenty of counter and cabinet space will please the gourmet of the family. A full bath and a utility room complete this floor. Upstairs, the sleeping zone is complete with two family bedrooms sharing a linen closet and a full hall bath, as well as a deluxe master suite. Features here include a private balcony, a walk-in closet and a dual-vanity bath.

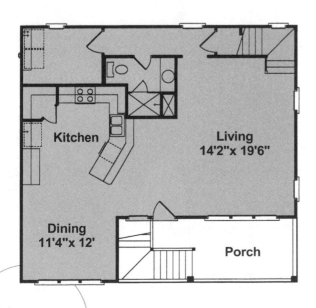

Kitchen

Living
14'2"x 19'6"

Dining
11'4"x 12'

Porch

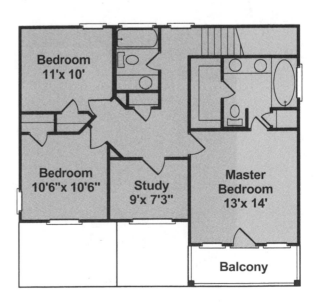

Bedroom
11'x 10'

Bedroom
10'6"x 10'6"

Study
9'x 7'3"

Master Bedroom
13'x 14'

Balcony

Design by
©Chatham Home Planning, Inc.

Design
R151

First Floor:
965 sq. ft.

Second Floor:
739 sq. ft.

Total:
1,704 sq. ft.

Width:
41'-4"

Depth:
30'-10"

With its elevated pier foundation, this home is well suited to coastal locations. Principal rooms are oriented toward the rear of the home for premium waterfront views. On the first floor, a two-story ceiling adds drama and space to the great room, which is open to the dining room and kitchen for a large gathering area. The great room, dining room and study/bedroom all open to the rear porch. Upstairs, a balcony overlooking the great room and foyer joins the master suite and a secondary bedroom and bath. The master suite features a cathedral ceiling, walk-in closet and its own private bath with separate tub and shower.

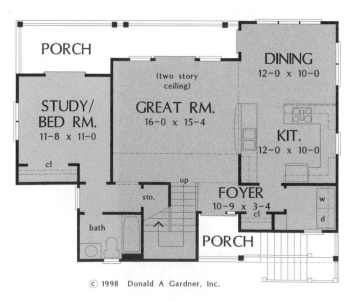

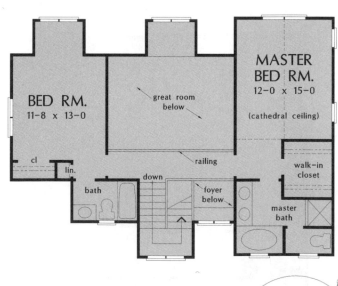

Design by

Donald A. Gardner Architects, Inc.

Design E159

First Floor:
907 sq. ft.

Second Floor:
872 sq. ft.

Total:
1,779 sq. ft.

○ **Width:**
34'-0"

Depth:
30'-0"

Two stories and still up on a pier foundation! A covered front porch leads to two sets of French doors—one to the spacious living room and one to the dining area. An L-shaped kitchen features a work-top island, a nearby utility room and plenty of counter and cabinet space. A sun room finishes off this floor with class. Upstairs, the sleeping zone consists of two family bedrooms—one with access to a balcony—a full bath and a master bedroom suite. Here, the homeowner will surely be pleased with a walk-in closet, a corner tub and a separate shower, as well as balcony access.

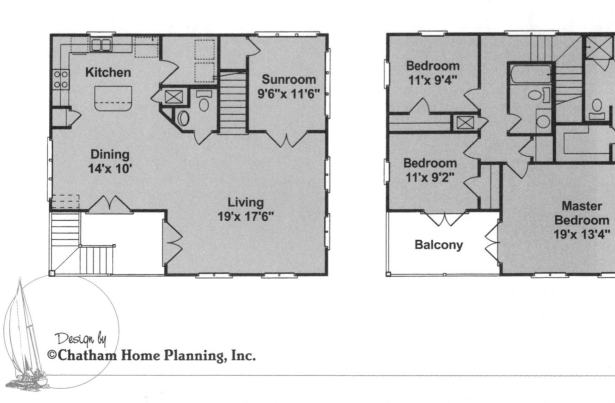

Kitchen

Sunroom
9'6"x 11'6"

Dining
14'x 10'

Living
19'x 17'6"

Bedroom
11'x 9'4"

Bedroom
11'x 9'2"

Balcony

Master
Bedroom
19'x 13'4"

Design by
©Chatham Home Planning, Inc.

Design
E172

First Floor:
1,623 sq. ft.

Second Floor:
978 sq. ft.

Total:
2,601 sq. ft.

Width:
48'-0"

Depth:
57'-0"

Offering a large wraparound porch, this fine two-story pier home is full of amenities. The living room has a warming fireplace and plenty of windows to enjoy the view. The galley kitchen features unique angles, with a large island/peninsula separating this room from the dining area. Two bedrooms share a bath and easy access to the laundry facilities. Upstairs, a lavish master bedroom suite is complete with a detailed ceiling, a private covered porch, a walk-in closet and a pampering bath. A secondary bedroom with a large walk-in closet finishes off this floor.

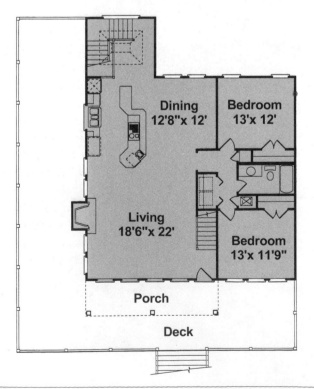

Dining
12'8"x 12'

Bedroom
13'x 12'

Living
18'6"x 22'

Bedroom
13'x 11'9"

Porch

Deck

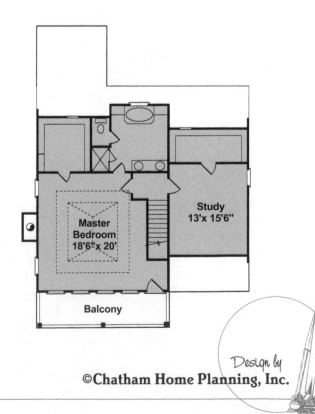

Master
Bedroom
18'6"x 20'

Study
13'x 15'6"

Balcony

©Chatham Home Planning, Inc.

Design by

Design E205

First Floor:
1,252 sq. ft.

Second Floor:
920 sq. ft.

Total:
2,172 sq. ft.

Width:
37'-0"

Depth:
46'-0"

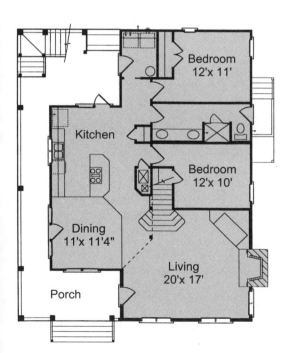

Bedroom
12'x 11'

Kitchen

Bedroom
12'x 10'

Dining
11'x 11'4"

Living
20'x 17'

Porch

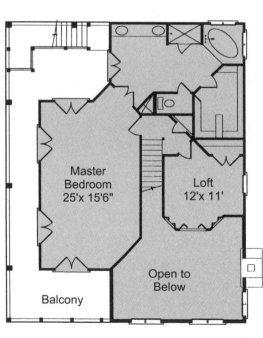

Master
Bedroom
25'x 15'6"

Loft
12'x 11'

Open to
Below

Balcony

Porches and balconies combine with the amenities inside this fine two-story home to provide a truly welcoming atmosphere. The foyer opens to the living room, where a fireplace and built-ins wait to greet family and visitors alike. The open kitchen offers a cooktop island and an adjacent dining area. Two bedrooms share a full bath and complete this floor. Upstairs, a lavish master suite reigns supreme. Here, the home-owner is pampered with a wraparound deck, walk-in closet, sumptuous bath and an adjacent loft—perfect for a computer room or home office.

Design by
©Chatham Home Planning, Inc.

Design
Y044

First Floor:
1,976 sq. ft.

Second Floor:
634 sq. ft.

Total:
2,610 sq. ft.

Width:
91'-10"

Depth:
54'-0"

This unique pier foundation home is sure to be an eye-catcher on any beachfront property. The bungalow-type roof adds a bit of rustic flavor, with its overhang also being useful in keeping the sun from the windows. With the bedrooms separated from the main living areas, there is truly a sense of privacy achieved. The living areas include a great room with a fireplace, a studio area with deck access, a dining area and an efficient kitchen full of amenities. Here, the family gourmet will be pleased with tons of counter and cabinet space and a wall of pantry space. The sleeping structure is accessible via an enclosed bridge. Here one can either go up to the lavish master suite—complete with a private covered deck, walk-in closet and deluxe bath—or downstairs to a huge bedroom. This room also has a private covered deck, walk-in closet and a private bath.

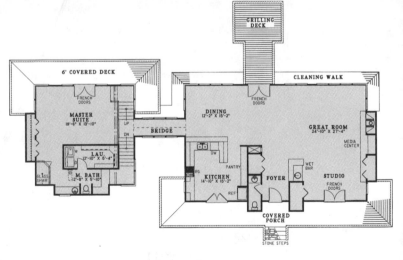

Front View

©Nelson Design Group, LLC

Design by

164

Design
E202

Square
Footage:
1,649

Width:
72'-0"

Depth:
54'-6"

The grand entry of this three-bedroom home is just the start of the appeal to be seen. The wraparound porch offers plenty of room for stargazing or enjoying ocean breezes. Inside, a spacious living room is highlighted by angled windows and a warming fireplace. The adjacent kitchen and dining area give this space an open, welcoming feeling. Separated for privacy, two family bedrooms share a bath on the right side of the home, while the master bedroom is located to the left of the home.

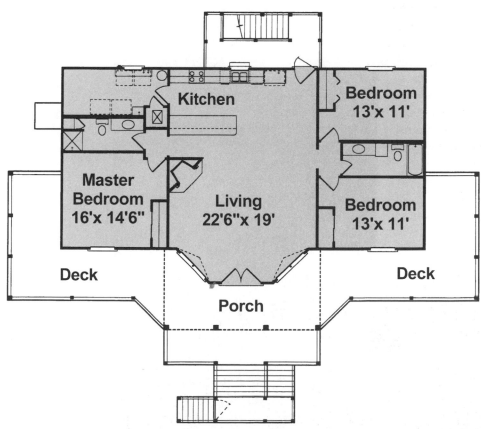

Kitchen

Bedroom
13' x 11'

Master
Bedroom
16' x 14'6"

Living
22'6" x 19'

Bedroom
13' x 11'

Deck

Deck

Porch

Design by
©Chatham Home Planning, Inc.

Design
E154

Square Footage: 1,520

Width: 40'-0"

Depth: 59'-0"

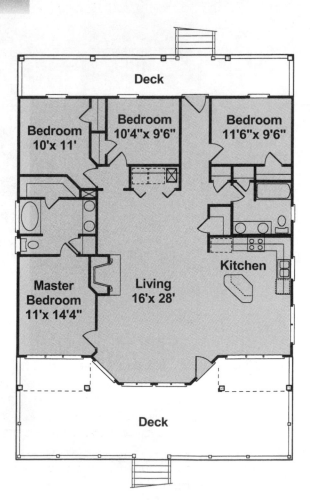

Deck

Bedroom 10'x 11'

Bedroom 10'4"x 9'6"

Bedroom 11'6"x 9'6"

Master Bedroom 11'x 14'4"

Living 16'x 28'

Kitchen

Deck

Size doesn't always predict amenities! This one-story pier foundation home is only 1,520 square feet, but it's packed with surprises. A skylight brings sunshine to the foyer, which leads to the spacious living room. Here, a huge wall of windows shows off the beach, while a fireplace offers warmth on cool winter evenings. The L-shaped kitchen features an angled work island and has easy access to the adjacent dining area. Three secondary bedrooms share a full bath and provide ample room for family or guests. The master bedroom is complete with a walk-in closet and a private bath.

Design by

©**Chatham Home Planning, Inc.**

Design 6617

First Floor: 1,189 sq. ft.

Second Floor: 575 sq. ft.

Total: 1,764 sq. ft.

Width: 46'-0"

Depth: 44'-6"

Photo by Oscar Thompson

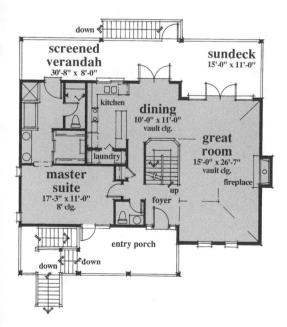

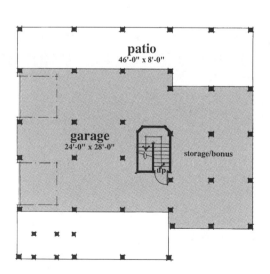

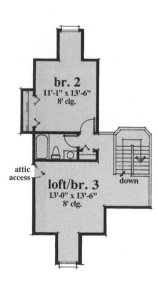

An abundance of porches and a deck encourage year-round indoor-outdoor relationships in this classic two-story home. The spacious living room, with its cozy fireplace, and the adjacent dining room both offer access to the screened porch/deck area. An efficient kitchen and nearby laundry room make chores easy. The private master suite offers access to the screened porch and leads into a relaxing master bath complete with a walk-in closet. Bedroom 2 shares the second floor with a full bath and a loft, which may be used as a third bedroom.

Design by
©The Sater Design Collection

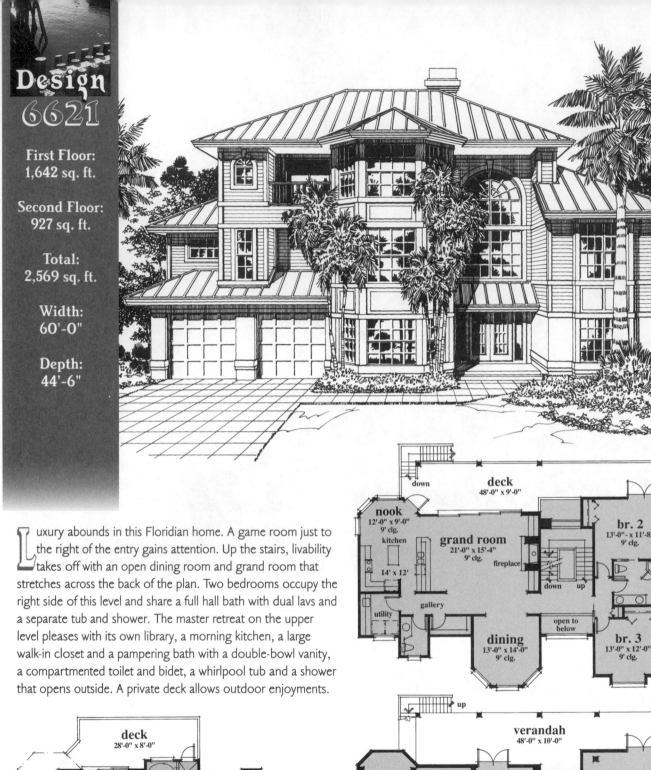

Design 6621

First Floor:
1,642 sq. ft.

Second Floor:
927 sq. ft.

Total:
2,569 sq. ft.

Width:
60'-0"

Depth:
44'-6"

Luxury abounds in this Floridian home. A game room just to the right of the entry gains attention. Up the stairs, livability takes off with an open dining room and grand room that stretches across the back of the plan. Two bedrooms occupy the right side of this level and share a full hall bath with dual lavs and a separate tub and shower. The master retreat on the upper level pleases with its own library, a morning kitchen, a large walk-in closet and a pampering bath with a double-bowl vanity, a compartmented toilet and bidet, a whirlpool tub and a shower that opens outside. A private deck allows outdoor enjoyments.

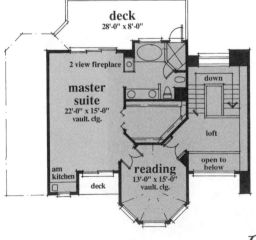

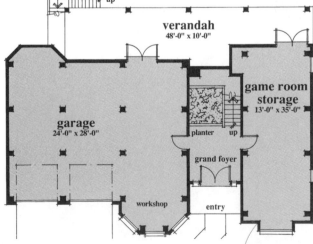

Design by
©The Sater Design Collection

Design
6619

First Floor:
2,725 sq. ft.

Second Floor:
1,418 sq. ft.

Total:
4,143 sq. ft.

Width:
61'-4"

Depth:
62'-0"

Florida living takes off in this grand pier design. A grand room gains attention as a superb entertaining area. A through-fireplace here connects this room to the dining room. Sets of sliding glass doors offer passage to an expansive rear deck. In the bayed study, quiet time is assured—or slip out onto the deck for a breather. A full bath connects the study and Bedroom 2. Bedroom 3 sits on the opposite side of the house and enjoys its own bath. The kitchen is fully functional with a large work island and a sunny connecting breakfast nook. Upstairs, the master bedroom suite is something to behold. His and Hers baths, a through-fireplace and access to an upper deck add character to this room. A guest bedroom suite with a bay window is located on the other side of the upper floor and will make visits a real pleasure.

Design by
©The Sater Design Collection

QUOTE ONE®

Cost to build? See page 198
to order complete cost estimate
to build this house in your area!

Design 7759

First Floor:
1,362 sq. ft.

Second Floor:
481 sq. ft.

Total:
1,843 sq. ft.

Width:
49'-4"

Depth:
44'-10"

B.NATHAN

©1998 Donald A. Gardner, Inc.

An enchanting wraparound porch, delightful dormers and bright bay windows create excitement inside and out for this coastal home. The large center dormer brightens the vaulted foyer, while the great room with cathedral ceiling enjoys added light from a trio of rear clerestory windows. A balcony dividing the second-floor bedrooms overlooks the great room and visually connects the two floors. The main suite is located on the first floor and features back-porch access, a walk-in closet and private bath with a garden tub and separate shower. The second-floor bedrooms, each with dormer alcoves, share a hall bath with dual-sink vanity.

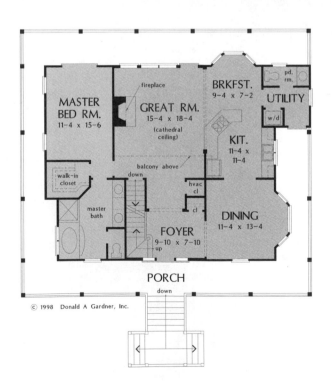

© 1998 Donald A Gardner, Inc.

Design by

Donald A. Gardner Architects, Inc.

BAREFOOT LUXURY

Lavish waterfront homes

Design T177 by Stephen Fuller. See page 27 for details

"The lake is calm,

the sun is low—

The whippoorwill

is chaunting slow—

And scarce a leaf

through the forest

is seen

To wave

in the breeze

its rich mantel

of green."

Chicomico

Design
A307

First Floor:
2,297 sq. ft.

Second Floor:
1,929 sq. ft.

Total:
4,226 sq. ft.

Width:
59'-2"

Depth:
49'-4"

Elegant twin staircases lead up to a grand portico on this fine two-story pier home. Double doors open to the foyer, which is flanked by a guest suite and a formal dining room. The spacious grand room just ahead features three sets of French doors to the rear deck as well as built-ins in one corner. Through double doors a cozy study awaits, with a warming fireplace and a pair of French doors to the deck. The guest suite offers a private bath and a walk-in closet. The U-shaped kitchen and adjacent breakfast and dining rooms fulfill all meal needs. Upstairs, the master suite is designed to pamper, with a sitting area, two walk-in closets and a lavish bath. Two secondary suites feature private baths and plenty of closet space.

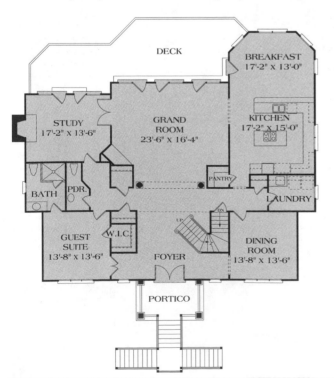

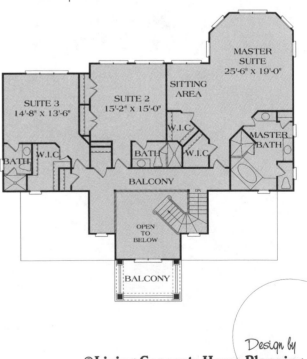

©Living Concepts Home Planning

Design by

Design
A225

First Floor:
3,329 sq. ft.

Second Floor:
1,485 sq. ft.

Total:
4,814 sq. ft.

Bonus Room:
300 sq. ft.

Width:
106'-6"

Depth:
89'-10"

In case you're not impressed by the covered drive, media room, walk-in pantry, ramada and four bedroom suites with private baths, this home offers a separate circular lanai topped by an evening deck that's overlooked by the Captain's quarters observation room. In addition, the master suite includes an exercise room and a curved lounge bay. The circle pattern continues in the study, which looks out to the ramada.

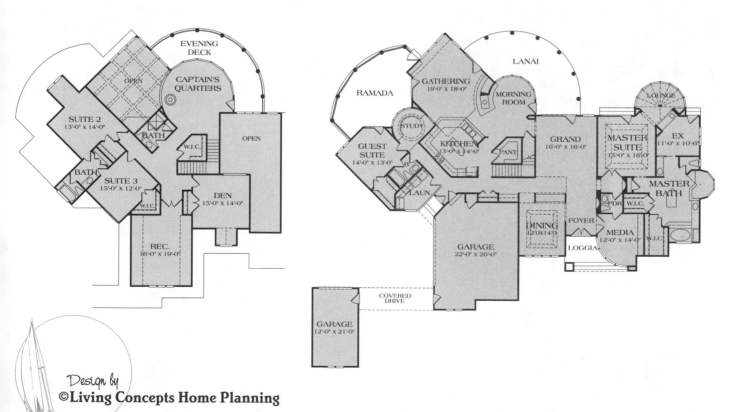

Design by
©Living Concepts Home Planning

Design
6697

First Floor:
1,642 sq. ft.

Second Floor:
927 sq. ft.

Total:
2,569 sq. ft.

Bonus Room:
849 sq. ft.

Width:
60'-0"

Depth:
44'-6"

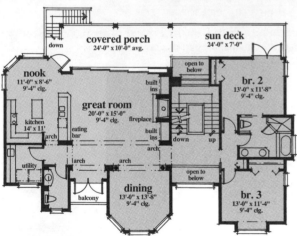

covered porch
24'-0" x 10'-0" avg.

sun deck
24'-0" x 7'-0"

nook
11'-0" x 8'-6"
9'-4" clg.

great room
20'-0" x 15'-0"
9'-4" clg.

kitchen
14' x 11'

br. 2
13'-0" x 11'-8"
9'-4" clg.

down

built ins

fireplace

built ins

eating bar

arch

down   up

arch

utility

arch   arch

balcony

dining
13'-0" x 13'-8"
9'-4" clg.

open to below

br. 3
13'-0" x 11'-4"
9'-4" clg.

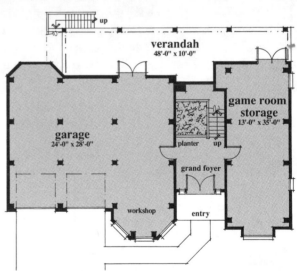

up

verandah
48'-0" x 10'-0"

garage
24'-0" x 28'-0"

game room storage
13'-0" x 35'-0"

planter   up

grand foyer

workshop

entry

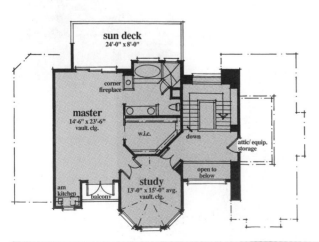

sun deck
24'-0" x 8'-0"

corner fireplace

master
14'-6" x 23'-6"
vault. clg.

w.i.c.

down

attic/ equip. storage

open to below

am kitchen

balcony

study
13'-0" x 15'-0" avg.
vault. clg.

Balconies and a three-story turret are stunning additions to this Gulf Coast design. Sliding glass doors open the great room to the rear covered porch and adjoining sun deck. A columned archway frames the dining room, located in the turret. The second floor, a homeowners' retreat, houses the master bedroom, sun deck, morning kitchen, a luxurious bath, balcony and study. The lower floor includes a game room and adds 849 square feet to the total.

Design by

©The Sater Design Collection

Design
6698

First Floor:
1,684 sq. ft.

Second Floor:
1,195 sq. ft.

Total:
2,879 sq. ft.

Bonus Room:
674 sq. ft.

Width:
45'-0"

Depth:
52'-0"

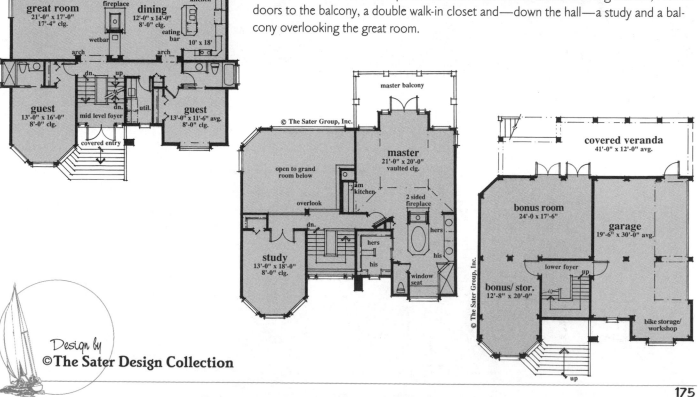

Asymmetrical rooflines set off a grand turret and a two-story bay that allow glorious views from the front of the home. Arch-top clerestory windows bring natural light into the great room, which shares a corner fireplace and a wet bar with the dining room. Two guest suites are located on this floor. A winding staircase leads to a luxurious master suite that shares a fireplace with the bath and includes a morning kitchen, French doors to the balcony, a double walk-in closet and—down the hall—a study and a balcony overlooking the great room.

Design by
©The Sater Design Collection

Design
Q435

First Floor:
2,473 sq. ft.

Second Floor:
2,686 sq. ft.

Total:
5,159 sq. ft.

Width:
57'-8"

Depth:
103'-6"

This unusual stucco-and-siding design opens with a grand portico to a foyer containing a volume ceiling that extends to the living room. A multi-paned transom lights the foyer and the open staircase beyond. The living room has a fireplace and then proceeds up a few steps to the dining room, with coffered ceiling and butler's pantry, which connects it to the gourmet kitchen. Cooks will love the wet bar in the butler's pantry, the walk-in food pantry, a wine cooler, a built-in desk and the center island with cooktop and salad sink. The attached hearth room has the requisite fireplace and three sets of French doors to the covered porch.

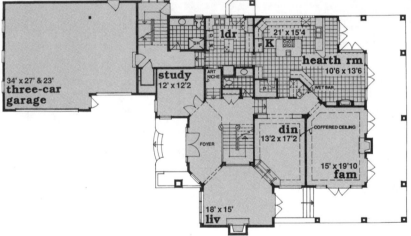

The family room sports a coffered ceiling and fireplace flanked by French doors. The second floor boasts four bedrooms, including a master suite with tray ceiling, covered deck and lavish bath. Two full baths serve the family bedrooms and a bonus room that might be used as an additional bedroom or hobby space.

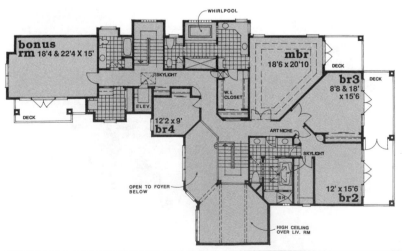

Design by
©Select Home Designs

176

Design
A217

First Floor:
2,547 sq. ft.

Second Floor:
1,637 sq. ft.

Total:
4,184 sq. ft.

Bonus Room:
802 sq. ft.

Width:
74'-0"

Depth:
95'-6"

The grand exterior of this home, with its multi-paned windows and huge Palladian over the entrance, holds an equally grand interior. The foyer has the dining room to the right, and opens to the two-story grand room. The circular morning room, with a bank of windows, joins the gathering room, which has a fireplace. The kitchen, with ample counter space and a pantry, easily serves everyone. The master suite is on this floor, with a huge master bath and windowed sitting area. Three additional suites are upstairs, as are the Captain's quarters, which are surrounded by windows and have access to the upper deck. A huge bonus room, for storage or a recreation room, is above the three-car garage.

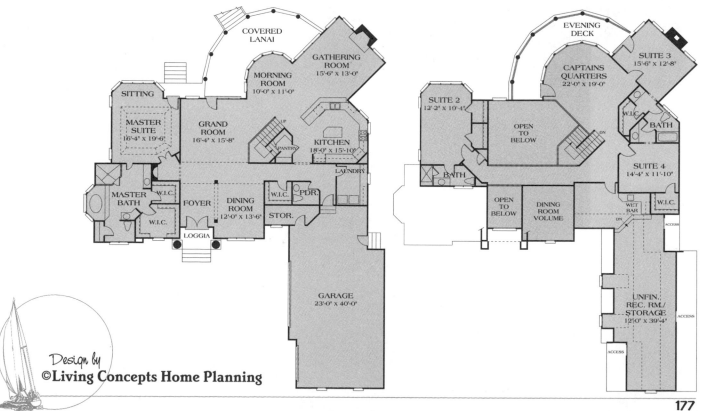

Design by
©Living Concepts Home Planning

Design
7530

First Floor:
2,709 sq. ft.

Second Floor:
2,321 sq. ft.

Total:
5,030 sq. ft.

Width:
121'-2"

Depth:
77'-7"

A huge foyer with a curved staircase welcomes you to this palatial four-bedroom home. On the main floor, you'll find the dining room, living room, den, family room, kitchen and dining nook, laundry room, two powder rooms, four-car garage and lap pool. Terraces wrap partially around the home. On the second floor, the master suite includes a sitting room, deck, walk-in closet and a compartmented bath. Three family bedrooms share two baths. The media room, also on the second floor, features a wet bar and overlooks the pool below.

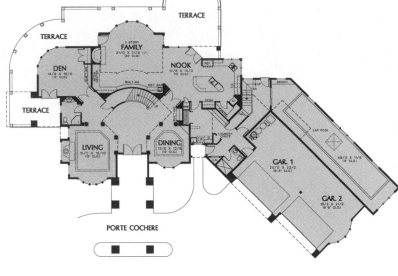

PORTE COCHERE

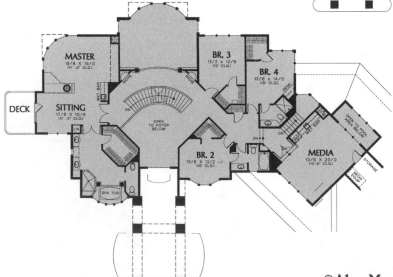

©Alan Mascord Design Associates, Inc.

Design by

Design
7506

First Floor:
2,035 sq. ft.

Second Floor:
1,543 sq. ft.

Total:
3,578 sq. ft.

Bonus Room:
366 sq. ft.

Width:
62'-0"

Depth:
76'-0"

Twin sets of columns usher one into the two-story foyer of this fine home. A quiet study to the left would make a good home office. Entertaining will truly be pleasant, with a formal living room—complete with fireplace—a formal dining room and a spacious family room all opening onto a large covered porch—perfect for catching the ocean breezes. Note the fireplace in the family room as well as the one on the porch. The kitchen will please the gourmet of the family, with its abundance of amenities. Upstairs, two family bedrooms share a full bath and access to a large bonus room. A guest room is nicely separate from the family rooms and offers a private bath. The lavish master suite is designed to pamper with a private deck, a huge walk-in closet and a deluxe bath.

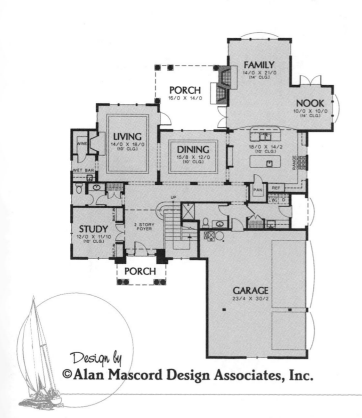

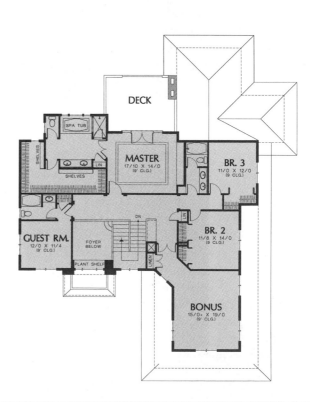

Design by
©Alan Mascord Design Associates, Inc.

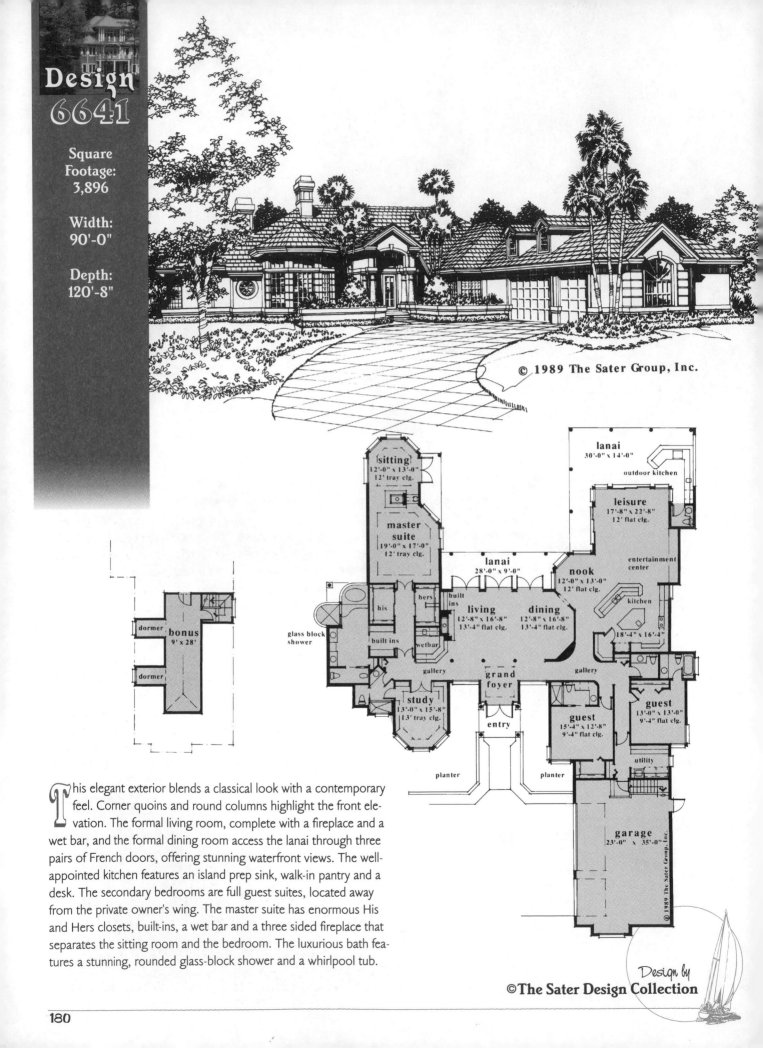

Design 6641

Square Footage: 3,896

Width: 90'-0"

Depth: 120'-8"

© 1989 The Sater Group, Inc.

Floor plan labels:

- sitting 12'-0" x 13'-0" 12' tray clg.
- master suite 19'-0" x 17'-0" 12' tray clg.
- lanai 30'-0" x 14'-0"
- outdoor kitchen
- leisure 17'-8" x 22'-8" 12' flat clg.
- entertainment center
- lanai 28'-0" x 9'-0"
- nook 12'-0" x 13'-0" 12' flat clg.
- his
- hers
- built ins
- kitchen
- living 12'-8" x 16'-8" 13'-4" flat clg.
- dining 12'-8" x 16'-8" 13'-4" flat clg.
- 18'-4" x 16'-4"
- glass block shower
- built ins
- wetbar
- gallery
- gallery
- grand foyer
- study 13'-0" x 15'-8" 13' tray clg.
- guest 15'-4" x 12'-8" 9'-4" clg.
- guest 13'-0" x 13'-0" 9'-4" flat clg.
- entry
- utility
- planter
- planter
- garage 23'-0" x 35'-0"
- dormer
- bonus 9' x 28'
- dormer

© 1989 The Sater Group, Inc.

This elegant exterior blends a classical look with a contemporary feel. Corner quoins and round columns highlight the front elevation. The formal living room, complete with a fireplace and a wet bar, and the formal dining room access the lanai through three pairs of French doors, offering stunning waterfront views. The well-appointed kitchen features an island prep sink, walk-in pantry and a desk. The secondary bedrooms are full guest suites, located away from the private owner's wing. The master suite has enormous His and Hers closets, built-ins, a wet bar and a three sided fireplace that separates the sitting room and the bedroom. The luxurious bath features a stunning, rounded glass-block shower and a whirlpool tub.

Design by
©The Sater Design Collection

Design
6636

Square Footage:
4,565

Width:
88'-0"

Depth:
95'-0"

built ins

guest
14'-4" x 14'-6"
tray clg.

books

entertainment center

leisure
25'-0" x 19'-10"
13'-4" flat clg.

fireplace

sitting

am kitchen

corner fireplace

master suite
17'-0" x 32'-0"
13'-4" flat clg.

nook
11'-0" x 11'-0"
13'-4" flat clg.

outdoor kitchen

curved glass

lanai

his

guest
12'-8" x 12'-4"
9'-4" flat clg.

kitchen

14'-0" x 18'-0"

living
15'-0" x 14'-0"
vaulted clg.

hers

sauna

utility

gallery

wetbar

exer.
10' x 14'

dining
11'-4" x 15'-0"
vaulted clg.

foyer

study
14'-1" x 20'-0"
13'-4" flat clg.

curved glass

garage
22'-8" x 30'-8"

entry

workbench

A free-standing entryway is the focal point of this luxurious residence. It has an arch motif that is carried through to the rear using a gable roof and a vaulted ceiling from the foyer out to the lanai. High ceilings are found throughout the home, creating a spacious atmosphere. The kitchen, which features a cooktop island and plenty of counter space, opens to the leisure area with a handy snack bar. Two guest suites with private baths are just off this casual living area. The master wing is truly pampering, stretching the entire length of the home. The suite has a large sitting area, a corner fireplace and a morning kitchen. The bath features an island vanity, a raised tub with a curved glass wall overlooking a private garden, a sauna and separate closets. An exercise room has a curved glass wall and a pocket door to the study, where a wet bar is ready to serve up refreshment. Outdoor living will be welcome, thanks to the lovely rear lanai and an outdoor kitchen.

Rear View

Design
A300

First Floor:
2,030 sq. ft.

Second Floor:
1,967 sq. ft.

Total:
3,997 sq. ft.

Bonus Room:
688 sq. ft.

Unfinished Area:
642 sq. ft.

Width:
80'-8"

Depth:
111'-8"

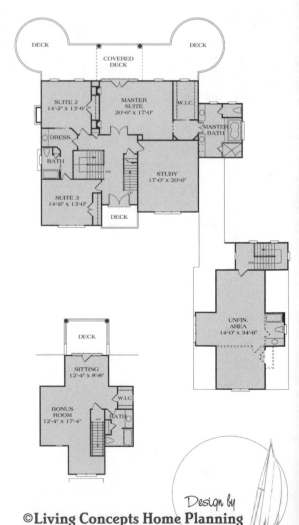

This Northwest Coastal/country-style home extends livability outside with its front and back porches and elevated deck—perfect for watching sunsets and catching ocean or lakeside breezes. The first floor flows from the open family room and breakfast nook to the kitchen with U-shaped counters. The dining room opens to the kitchen and the foyer. In the front is a guest suite with a private bath. Upstairs, the spacious master suite has a walk-in closet and access to the deck. The family bedrooms share a bath. To the right is a study. The garage is attached to the main house by a breezeway and above it is an unfinished area that can be converted to an apartment sometime in the future. The full bath is already installed.

©**Living Concepts Home Planning**

Design X059

Main Level:
2,103 sq. ft.

Lower Level:
1,130 sq. ft.

Basement Level:
774 sq. ft.

Total:
4,007 sq. ft.

Width:
70'-0"

Depth:
44'-0"

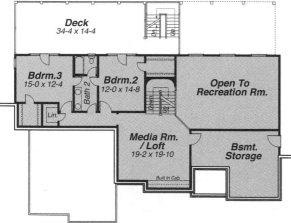

Deck
34-4 x 14-4

Bdrm.3
15-0 x 12-4

Bdrm.2
12-0 x 14-8

Bath 2

Lin.

Open To Recreation Rm.

Media Rm. / Loft
19-2 x 19-10

Bsmt. Storage

Built In Cab.

The simple one-story look to the front of this wonderful home will add delight to the surprised looks you'll see when the rest of the house unfolds in front of your guests. From the foyer, a formal dining room and a formal living room can be seen. The master suite—located for privacy—is just to the left and is full of amenities. A fireplace warms the family room, which is convenient to the efficient kitchen and bayed breakfast area. The master suite, dining room and family room all have access to the large sun deck that stretches across the rear of the home. Down one level are two family bedrooms sharing a bath, a media/loft room and an overlook to the lower recreation room. Go down yet another level and you will find tons of basement storage and a large recreation room complete with a wet bar and a covered patio.

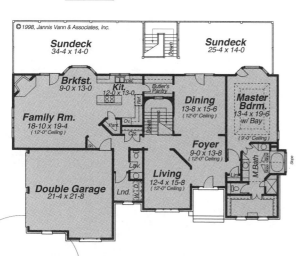

© 1998, Jannis Vann & Associates, Inc.

Sundeck
34-4 x 14-0

Sundeck
25-4 x 14-0

Brkfst.
9-0 x 13-0

Kit.
12-0 x 13-0

Butler's Pantry

Dining
13-8 x 15-6
(12'-0" Ceiling)

Master Bdrm.
13-4 x 19-6
w/ Bay

Family Rm.
18-10 x 19-4
(12'-0" Ceiling)

Pant.

Foyer
9-0 x 13-8
(12'-0" Ceiling)

(9'-0" Ceiling)

M.Bath

Double Garage
21-4 x 21-8

Lav.

Lnd.

Living
12-4 x 15-8
(12'-0" Ceiling)

Lin.

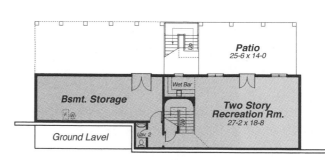

Patio
25-6 x 14-0

Wet Bar

Bsmt. Storage

Two Story Recreation Rm.
27-2 x 18-8

Lav. 2

Ground Level

Design by
© **Jannis Vann & Associates, Inc.**

183

Design A203

First Floor:
2,202 sq. ft.

Second Floor:
1,355 sq. ft.

Total:
3,557 sq. ft.

Bonus Room:
523 sq. ft.

Width:
66'-0"

Depth:
65'-10"

Columns and arches distinguish the front porch of this attractive shingle-sided, waterfront home. Two sets of French doors lead to the deck or terrace from the gathering room, which has a fireplace. The foyer includes a convenient powder room for guests. The efficient kitchen will easily serve a quiet dinner for two in the adjacent breakfast nook or a grand dinner party in the nearby formal dining room. A central upper-level room provides space for study or play. Bonus space on the upper level can add 523 square feet.

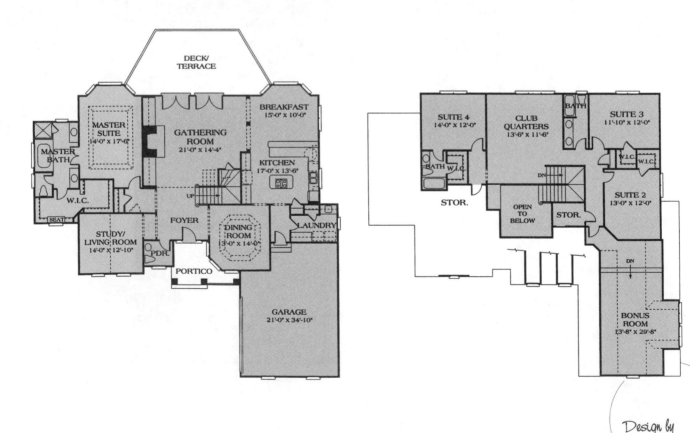

©Living Concepts Home Planning

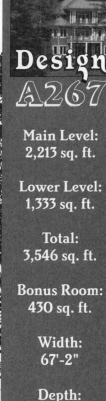

Design
A267

Main Level:
2,213 sq. ft.

Lower Level:
1,333 sq. ft.

Total:
3,546 sq. ft.

Bonus Room:
430 sq. ft.

Width:
67'-2"

Depth:
93'-1"

Interesting window treatments highlight this stone-and-shake facade, but don't overlook the columned porch to the left of the portico. Arches outline the formal dining room and the family room, both of which are convenient to the island kitchen. Household chores are made easier by the placement of a pantry, a powder room, a laundry room and an office between the kitchen and entrances to a side porch and the garage. If your goal is relaxing, the breakfast room, a screened porch and a covered deck are also nearby. The pampering master suite is to the left of the main level, with three more bedrooms and a recreation room on the lower level. A bonus room above the garage receives natural light from a dormer window.

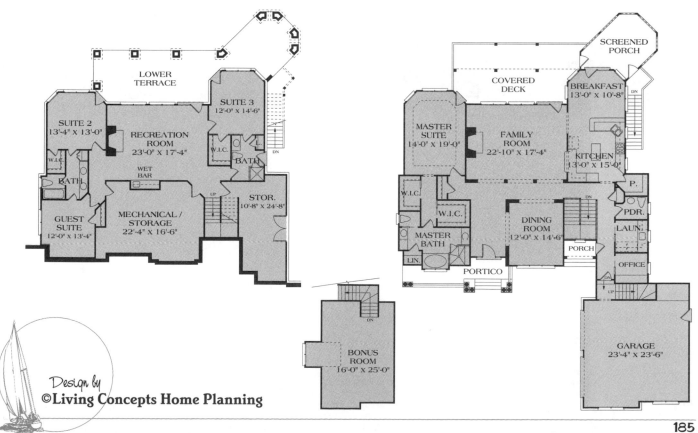

Design by
©Living Concepts Home Planning

Design
Y048

Main Level:
2,235 sq. ft.

Lower Level:
1,250 sq. ft.

Total:
3,485 sq. ft.

Width:
78'-2"

Depth:
53'-8"

Front View

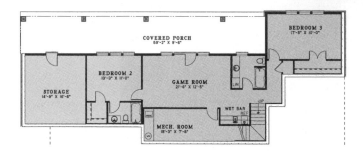

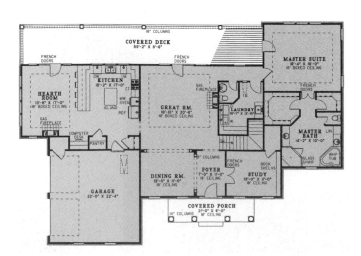

Looking like a classy formal one-story home, visitors will be pleasantly surprised at the space available—on two levels! The main level consists of a formal dining room to the left of the foyer, defined by columns, a cozy study with built-in bookshelves and a spacious great room with a gas fireplace and French door access to the rear covered deck. Also on this level, the U-shaped kitchen is sure to please with a work island, a built-in desk, a snack-bar peninsula and an adjacent hearth room. Located on this level for privacy is the lavish master suite. From the two walk-in closets, corner shower and whirlpool tub and rear-deck access, this suite is a delight to relax in. Downstairs, the lower level is complete with two large bedrooms, each with a walk-in closet, two full baths, a huge game room with outdoor access and a wet bar. Note all of the storage available down here too. Please specify basement, crawlspace, slab or block foundation when ordering.

©Nelson Design Group, LLC

Design
Y049

Main Level:
3,364 sq. ft.

Upper Level:
1,929 sq. ft.

Lower Level:
1,540 sq. ft.

Total:
6,833 sq. ft.

Width:
88'-8"

Depth:
70'-5"

Design by
© **Nelson Design Group, LLC**

Looks can be deceiving! Though this fine home gives the impression of a one-story, in truth there are three levels of comfort to be found—and three levels of outdoor access to enjoy waterfront views. Inside, the great room offers a vaulted ceiling, built-ins and a stone fireplace along with French door access to one of two screened porches. The U-shaped kitchen is full of amenities, including an adjacent hearth room with a gas fireplace. A hobby/play room is also nearby with a full bath available. The master suite is lavish with a bay window and deluxe bath. A den/study and a cozy sitting area share a through-fireplace and access to the screened porch. The upper level consists of two spacious bedroom suites—each with a fireplace, private deck, walk-in closet and private bath. The lower level is complete with a game room/sitting area, a summer kitchen, two full baths, two bedrooms (or make one a media room) and tons of storage. Please specify basement, crawlspace, slab or block foundation when ordering.

Rear View

Design
Y051

First Floor:
2,687 sq. ft.

Second Floor:
342 sq. ft.

Total:
3,029 sq. ft.

Width:
73'-0"

Depth:
69'-4"

Front View

A perfect lakeside home, this fine four-bedroom home offers plenty of outdoor access. The main floor starts with an efficient kitchen to the left of the foyer—complete with a large island bar and lots of counter and cabinet space. The sunken and vaulted great room is just ahead and features exposed wood trusses, a fireplace and circular stairs to the spacious loft. All four large bedrooms have private baths and lots of closet space. Bedrooms 3 and 4 offer rear-porch access. Please specify slab or crawlspace foundation when ordering.

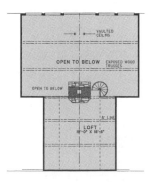

Design by

Design
7441

Main Level:
2,057 sq. ft.

Lower Level:
1,373 sq. ft.

Total:
3,430 sq. ft.

Width:
52'-0"

Depth:
71'-0"

Multi-pane windows, a sloping, lakeside lot and fine details are what make this home a true gem. Inside, a cozy den with double doors opens off the foyer. A spacious great room with a tray ceiling and a fireplace is near the formal dining room and the island kitchen. For dining alfresco, the casual dining nook offers direct access to the deck. A lavish master bedroom is located to the rear of the main level and is enhanced by a walk-in closet and an amenity-filled bath. A secondary bedroom completes this level. Downstairs, two more family bedrooms share a full bath and a large games room with a fireplace.

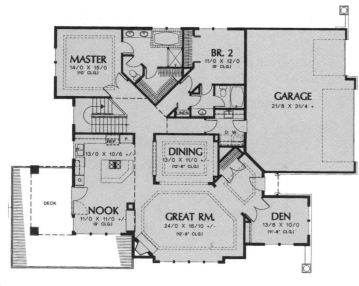

Design by
© Alan Mascord Design Associates, Inc.

First Floor:
2,033 sq. ft.

Second Floor:
1,116 sq. ft.

Total:
3,149 sq. ft.

Width:
71'-0"

Depth:
56'-0"

This large, Southern-style home offers luxury to spare, inside and out. Decorative columns and tall, arched windows along a raised porch welcome guests and introduce a grand, two-story foyer. Custom arches define both the entry and the great room, and maximize views. Picture the central fireplace glowing between graceful French doors, which open to a rear porch and deck—perfect for watching sunsets or catching lakeside breezes.

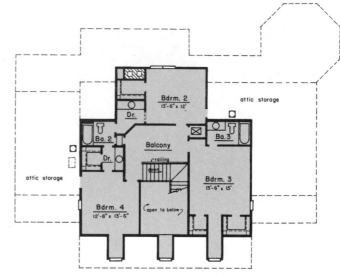

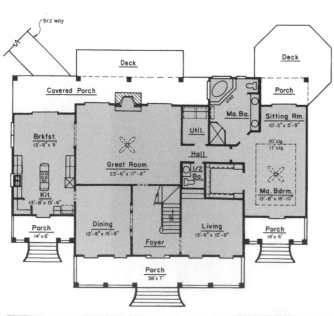

Luxury abounds in the opulent master suite, complete with a sitting room that leads to a private rear porch and deck, a separate front porch and a master bath with a corner whirlpool tub. The gourmet kitchen and adjoining breakfast area share a private porch as well. Upstairs, a hall balcony connects three family bedrooms and two full baths. Please specify crawlspace or slab foundation when ordering.

Design by

©**Chatham Home Planning, Inc.**

Design
Y050

Main Level:
2,711 sq. ft.

Lower Level:
948 sq. ft.

Total:
3,659 sq. ft.

Width:
122'-10"

Depth:
75'-5"

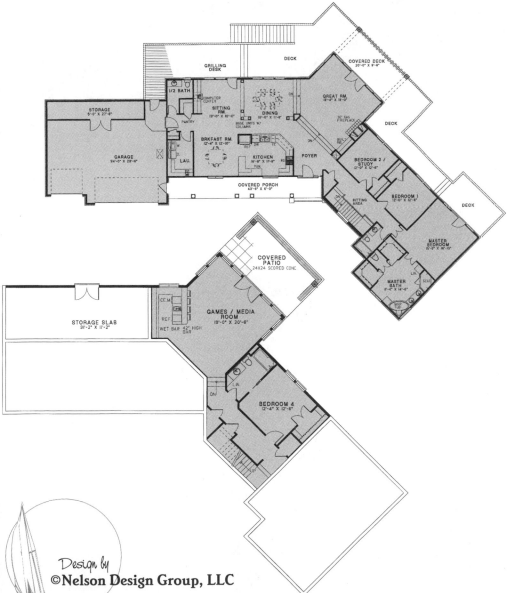

Spacious, attractive and perfect for lakeside living, this home is sure to please. A sunken great room features a warming fireplace and access to the rear covered deck. The efficient kitchen offers a breakfast room as well as easy access to the formal dining room. A sitting room nearby is complete with a built-in computer desk area. The lavish master suite is at the far right end of the home, and includes two walk-in closets, a lavish bath and direct access to a rear deck. Two family bedrooms and a full bath complete this level. Downstairs, a third family bedroom features a walk-in closet and a nearby full bath—perfect for a guest suite. This level is completed by a large games/media room, an extensive wet bar and outdoor access. Please specify crawlspace or slab foundation when ordering.

Design 3575

L

First Floor:
1,650 sq. ft.

Second Floor:
628 sq. ft.

Lower Floor:
977 sq. ft.

Total:
3,255 sq. ft.

Width:
52'-0"

Depth:
60'-0"

Front View

This contemporary design accommodates lakeside lots well with its lower-level living area. The guest bedroom located here accesses a full bath with an exercise room nearby. Also notable about this area is the activities room with its raised-hearth fireplace. A spacious, two-story gathering room with a large fireplace and a balcony defines the main floor. A formal dining room, also with a balcony, connects to the breakfast room and to the modern kitchen. The master bedroom, with its private bath and whirlpool tub, is also on this floor, with the laundry room conveniently nearby. Upstairs, two family bedrooms—each with its own balcony—share a full hall bath.

QUOTE ONE®
Cost to build? See page 198 to order complete cost estimate to build this house in your area!

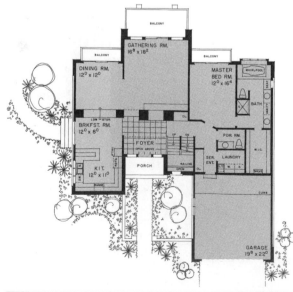

Design by
©Home Planners

First Floor:
1,096 sq. ft.

Second Floor:
1,115 sq. ft.

Lower Floor:
1,104 sq. ft.

Total:
3,315 sq. ft.

Width:
40'-0"

Depth:
58'-0"

Rear View

A splendidly symmetrical plan, this clean-lined, open-planned contemporary is a great place for the outdoor minded. A gathering room (with fireplace), dining room and breakfast room all lead out to a deck off the main level. Similarly, the lower-level activity room (another fireplace), hobby room and guest bedroom contain separate doors to the backyard terrace. Upstairs are three bedrooms, including a master suite with through-fireplace, private balcony, walk-in closet, dressing room and whirlpool tub.

QUOTE ONE®

Cost to build? See page 198 to order complete cost estimate to build this house in your area!

Design by
©**Home Planners**

Design
3361

L

Main Level:
3,548 sq. ft.

Lower Level:
1,036 sq. ft.

Total:
4,584 sq. ft.

Width:
74'-0"

Depth:
68'-8"

QUOTE ONE®
Cost to build? See page 198
to order complete cost estimate
to build this house in your area!

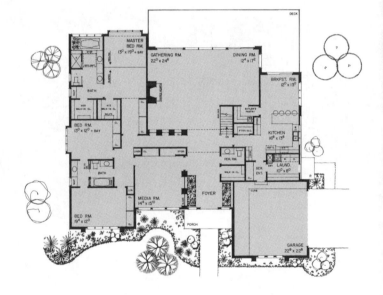

Here's a hillside haven that can easily accommodate the largest of families if necessary. It's perfect for both formal and informal occasions. Straight back from the foyer is a grand gathering room/dining room combination. It is complemented by the breakfast room and a front-facing media room. This level is complete with two family bedrooms and a lavish master suite. The lower level features a third family bedroom—or make it the guest suite—and a huge activities room with a warming fireplace and easy outdoor access. Note the full deck on the main level—perfect for watching sunsets over the water.

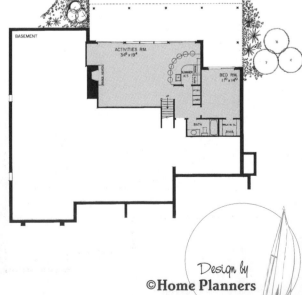

Front View

Design by
©Home Planners

Design
3360

L

Main Level:
2,673 sq. ft.

Lower Level:
1,389 sq. ft.

Total:
4,062 sq. ft.

Width:
60'-0"

Depth:
72'-0"

This plan has the best of both worlds—a traditional exterior and a modern, multi-level floor plan. The central foyer routes traffic effectively to all areas: the kitchen, gathering room, sleeping area and media room. The master suite features a luxurious bath and His and Hers walk-in closets. A large deck is accessible from the master bedroom as well as the gathering room. The lower level can be developed now or later. Plans include space for a summer kitchen, activities room and bedroom with full bath.

Rear View

QUOTE ONE®
Cost to build? See page 198 to order complete cost estimate to build this house in your area!

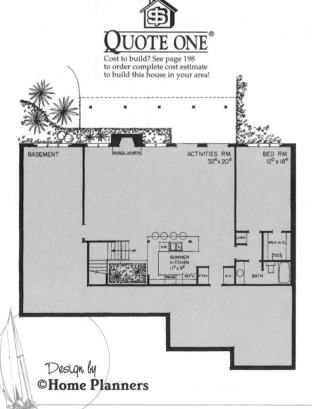

Design by
©**Home Planners**

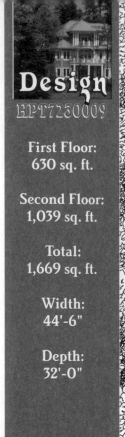

Design
HPT7230009

First Floor:
630 sq. ft.

Second Floor:
1,039 sq. ft.

Total:
1,669 sq. ft.

Width:
44'-6"

Depth:
32'-0"

This cozy design may look small, but the interior provides all the amenities an owner would want. A covered porch leads to a vaulted dining area, directly left of the island kitchen, complete with plenty of counter space and a pantry. The vaulted living room is graced with a fireplace, perfect for chilly evenings. The first-floor vaulted master suite enjoys a linen closet, large walk-in closet, tub and separate shower. Two additional bedrooms sharing a hall bath reside on the first floor. Bedroom 2 boasts a desk/seat area, perfect for studying.

BR. 2
10/0 X 11/0
(9' CLG.)

DESK OR SEAT

GARAGE
12/10 X 28/10

BR. 3
10/6 X 11/4
(9' CLG.)

VAULTED
DINING
11/0 X 14/0

DW

PAN. R

DN.

VAULTED
PORCH
11/0 X 10/6

VAULTED
LIVING
17/8 X 15/10

VAULTED
MASTER
13/0 X 14/8 + BAY

LINEN

SHLVS

Design by

©**Alan Mascord Design Associates, Inc.**

LET US SHOW YOU OUR HOME BLUEPRINT PACKAGE.

BUILDING A HOME? PLANNING A HOME?
OUR BLUEPRINT PACKAGE HAS NEARLY EVERYTHING YOU NEED TO GET THE JOB DONE RIGHT,

whether you're working on your own or with help from an architect, designer, builder or subcontractors. Each Blueprint Package is the result of many hours of work by licensed architects or professional designers.

QUALITY

Hundreds of hours of painstaking effort have gone into the development of your blueprint set. Each home has been quality-checked by professionals to insure accuracy and buildability.

VALUE

Because we sell in volume, you can buy professional quality blueprints at a fraction of their development cost. With our plans, your dream home design costs substantially less than the fees charged by architects.

SERVICE

Once you've chosen your favorite home plan, you'll receive fast, efficient service whether you choose to mail or fax your order to us or call us toll free at 1-800-521-6797. For customer service, call toll free 1-888-690-1116.

SATISFACTION

Over 50 years of service to satisfied home plan buyers provide us unparalleled experience and knowledge in producing quality blueprints.

ORDER TOLL FREE
1-800-521-6797

After you've looked over our Blueprint Package and Important Extras, call toll free on our Blueprint Hotline: 1-800-521-6797, for current pricing and availability prior to mailing the order form on page 205. We're ready and eager to serve you. For customer service, call toll free 1-888-690-1116.

Each set of blueprints is an interrelated collection of detail sheets which includes components such as floor plans, interior and exterior elevations, dimensions, cross-sections, diagrams and notations. These sheets show exactly how your house is to be built.

SETS MAY INCLUDE:

FRONTAL SHEET
This artist's sketch of the exterior of the house gives you an idea of how the house will look when built and landscaped. Large floor plans show all levels of the house and provide an overview of your new home's livability, as well as a handy reference for deciding on furniture placement.

FOUNDATION PLANS
This sheet shows the foundation layout including support walls, excavated and unexcavated areas, if any, and foundation notes. If slab construction rather than basement, the plan shows footings and details for a monolithic slab. This page, or another in the set, may include a sample plot plan for locating your house on a building site.

DETAILED FLOOR PLANS
These plans show the layout of each floor of the house. Rooms and interior spaces are carefully dimensioned and keys are given for cross-section details provided later in the plans. The positions of electrical outlets and switches are shown.

HOUSE CROSS-SECTIONS
Large-scale views show sections or cut-aways of the foundation, interior walls, exterior walls, floors, stairways and roof details. Additional cross-sections may show important changes in floor, ceiling or roof heights or the relationship of one level to another. Extremely valuable for construction, these sections show exactly how the various parts of the house fit together.

INTERIOR ELEVATIONS
Many of our drawings show the design and placement of kitchen and bathroom cabinets, laundry areas, fireplaces, bookcases and other built-ins. Little "extras," such as mantelpiece and wainscoting drawings, plus molding sections, provide details that give your home that custom touch.

EXTERIOR ELEVATIONS
These drawings show the front, rear and sides of your house and give necessary notes on exterior materials and finishes. Particular attention is given to cornice detail, brick and stone accents or other finish items that make your home unique.

IMPORTANT EXTRAS TO DO THE JOB RIGHT!

INTRODUCING EIGHT IMPORTANT

PLANNING AND CONSTRUCTION AIDS DEVELOPED BY

OUR PROFESSIONALS TO HELP YOU SUCCEED IN YOUR HOME-BUILDING PROJECT

MATERIALS LIST

(Note: Because of the diversity of local building codes, our Materials List does not include mechanical materials.)

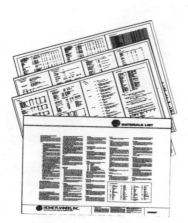

For many of the designs in our portfolio, we offer a customized materials take-off that is invaluable in planning and estimating the cost of your new home. This Materials List outlines the quantity, type and size of materials needed to build your house (with the exception of mechanical system items). Included are framing lumber, windows and doors, kitchen and bath cabinetry, rough and finish hardware, and much more. This handy list helps you or your builder cost out materials and serves as a reference sheet when you're compiling bids. A Materials List cannot be ordered before blueprints are ordered.

SPECIFICATION OUTLINE

This valuable 16-page document is critical to building your house correctly. Designed to be filled in by you or your builder, this book lists 166 stages or items crucial to the building process. It provides a comprehensive review of the construction process and helps in choosing materials. When combined with the blueprints, a signed contract, and a schedule, it becomes a legal document and record for the building of your home.

QUOTE ONE®

SUMMARY COST REPORT   **MATERIALS COST REPORT**

A product for estimating the cost of building select designs, the Quote One® system is available in two separate stages: The Summary Cost Report and the Materials Cost Report.

The **Summary Cost Report** is the first stage in the package and shows the total cost per square foot for your chosen home in your zip-code area and then breaks that cost down into various categories showing the costs for building materials, labor and installation. The report includes three grades: Budget, Standard and Custom. These reports allow you to evaluate your building budget and compare the costs of building a variety of homes in your area.

Make even more informed decisions about your home-building project with the second phase of our package, our **Materials Cost Report.** This tool is invaluable in planning and estimating the cost of your new home. The material and installation (labor and equipment) cost is shown for each of over 1,000 line items provided in the Materials List (Standard grade), which is included when you purchase this estimating tool. It allows you to determine building costs for your specific zip-code area and for your chosen home design. Space is allowed for additional estimates from contractors and subcontractors, such as for mechanical materials, which are not included in our packages. This invaluable tool includes a Materials List. A Materials Cost Report cannot be ordered before blueprints are ordered. Call for details. In addition, ask about our Home Planners Estimating Package.

If you are interested in a plan that is not indicated as Quote One®, please call and ask our sales reps. They will be happy to verify the status for you. To order these invaluable reports, use the order form on page 205 or call 1-800-521-6797 for availability.

CONSTRUCTION INFORMATION

IF YOU WANT TO KNOW MORE ABOUT TECHNIQUES— and deal more confidently with subcontractors — we offer these useful sheets. Each set is an excellent tool that will add to your understanding of these technical subjects. These helpful details provide general construction information and are not specific to any single plan.

PLUMBING
The Blueprint Package includes locations for all the plumbing fixtures, including sinks, lavatories, tubs, showers, toilets, laundry trays and water heaters. However, if you want to know more about the complete plumbing system, these Plumbing Details will prove very useful. Prepared to meet requirements of the National Plumbing Code, these fact-filled sheets give general information on pipe schedules, fittings, sump-pump details, water-softener hookups, septic system details and much more. Sheets also include a glossary of terms.

ELECTRICAL
The locations for every electrical switch, plug and outlet are shown in your Blueprint Package. However, these Electrical Details go further to take the mystery out of household electrical systems. Prepared to meet requirements of the National Electrical Code, these comprehensive drawings come packed with helpful information, including wire sizing, switch-installation schematics, cable-routing details, appliance wattage, doorbell hook-ups, typical service panel circuitry and much more. A glossary of terms is also included.

CONSTRUCTION
The Blueprint Package contains information an experienced builder needs to construct a particular house. However, it doesn't show all the ways that houses can be built, nor does it explain alternate construction methods. To help you understand how your house will be built—and offer additional techniques—this set of Construction Details depicts the materials and methods used to build foundations, fireplaces, walls, floors and roofs. Where appropriate, the drawings show acceptable alternatives.

MECHANICAL
These Mechanical Details contain fundamental principles and useful data that will help you make informed decisions and communicate with subcontractors about heating and cooling systems. Drawings contain instructions and samples that allow you to make simple load calculations, and preliminary sizing and costing analysis. Covered are the most commonly used systems from heat pumps to solar fuel systems. The package is filled with illustrations and diagrams to help you visualize components and how they relate to one another.

PLAN-A-HOME®

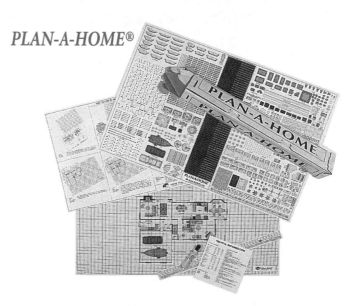

PLAN-A-HOME® is an easy-to-use tool that helps you design a new home, arrange furniture in a new or existing home, or plan a remodeling project. Each package contains:

✓ **More than 700 reusable peel-off planning symbols** on a self-stick vinyl sheet, including walls, windows, doors, all types of furniture, kitchen components, bath fixtures and many more.

✓ **A reusable, transparent, ¼" scale planning grid** that matches the scale of actual working drawings (¼" equals one foot). This grid provides the basis for house layouts of up to 140' x 92'.

✓ **Tracing paper** and a protective sheet for copying or transferring your completed plan.

✓ **A felt-tip pen**, with water-soluble ink that wipes away quickly.

PLAN-A-HOME® lets you lay out areas as large as a 7,500 square foot, six-bedroom, seven-bath house.

To Order, Call Toll Free
1-800-521-6797

After you've looked over our Blueprint Package and Important Extras on these pages, call toll free on our Blueprint Hotline: 1-800-521-6797 for current pricing and availability prior to mailing the order form on page 205. We're ready and eager to serve you. For customer service, call toll free 1-888-690-1116.

THE DECK BLUEPRINT PACKAGE

Many of the homes in this book can be enhanced with a professionally designed Home Planners Deck Plan. Those home plans highlighted with a **D** have a matching Deck Plan, sold separately, which includes a Deck Plan Frontal Sheet, Deck Framing and Floor Plans, Deck Elevations and a Deck Materials List. A Standard Deck Details Package, also available, provides all the how-to information necessary for building *any* deck. Our Complete Deck Building Package contains one set of Custom Deck Plans of your choice, plus one set of Standard Deck Building Details, all for one low price. Our plans and details are carefully prepared in an easy-to-understand format that will guide you through every stage of your deck-building project. This page shows a sample of Deck layouts to match your favorite house. See page 201 for prices and ordering information.

THE LANDSCAPE BLUEPRINT PACKAGE

For the homes marked with an **L** in this book, Home Planners has created a front-yard Landscape Plan that matches or is complementary in design to the house plan. These comprehensive blueprint packages include a Frontal Sheet, Plan View, Regionalized Plant & Materials List, a sheet on Planting and Maintaining Your Landscape, Zone Maps and Plant Size and Description Guide. These plans will help you achieve professional results, adding value and enjoyment to your property for years to come. Each set of blueprints is a full 18" x 24" in size with clear, complete instructions and easy-to-read type. A sample Landscape Plan is shown below.

CONTEMPORARY LEISURE DECK
Deck ODA021

CAPE COD COTTAGE
Landscape OLA003

Regional Order Map

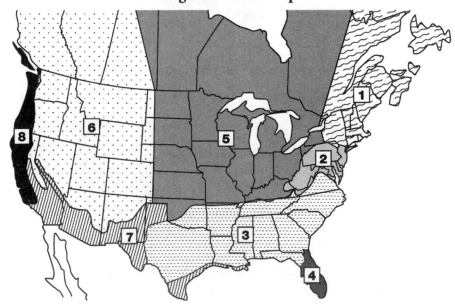

Most Landscape Plans are available with a Plant & Materials List adapted by horticultural experts to 8 different regions of the country. Please specify the Geographic Region when ordering your plan. See pages 201-203 for prices, ordering information and regional availability.

Region	1	Northeast
Region	2	Mid-Atlantic
Region	3	Deep South
Region	4	Florida & Gulf Coast
Region	5	Midwest
Region	6	Rocky Mountains
Region	7	Southern California & Desert Southwest
Region	8	Northern California & Pacific Northwest

HOUSE BLUEPRINT PRICE SCHEDULE

Prices guaranteed through December 31, 2002

TIERS	1-SET STUDY PACKAGE	4-SET BUILDING PACKAGE	8-SET BUILDING PACKAGE	1-SET REPRODUCIBLE
P1	$20	$50	$90	$140
P2	$40	$70	$110	$160
P3	$70	$100	$140	$190
P4	$100	$130	$170	$220
P5	$140	$170	$210	$270
P6	$180	$210	$250	$310
A1	$440	$480	$520	$660
A2	$480	$520	$560	$720
A3	$520	$560	$600	$780
A4	$565	$605	$645	$850
C1	$610	$655	$700	$915
C2	$655	$700	$745	$980
C3	$700	$745	$790	$1050
C4	$750	$795	$840	$1125
L1	$825	$875	$925	$1240
L2	$900	$950	$1000	$1340
L3	$1000	$1095	$1100	$1500
L4	$1100	$1150	$1200	$1650

OPTIONS FOR PLANS IN TIERS A1–L4

Additional Identical Blueprints
in same order for "A1–L4" price plans ....$50 per set
Reverse Blueprints (mirror image)
with 4- or 8-set order for "A1–L4" plans..$50 fee per order
Specification Outlines..$10 each
Materials Lists for "A1–C3" plans ....$60 each
Materials Lists for "C4–L4" plans...$70 each

IMPORTANT NOTES

The 1-set study package is marked "not for construction."
Prices for 4- or 8-set Building Packages honored only at time of original order.
Some foundations carry a $225 surcharge.
Right-reading reverse blueprints, if available, will incur a $165 surcharge.
Additional identical blueprints may be purchased within 60 days of original order.

OPTIONS FOR PLANS IN TIERS P1–P6

Additional Identical Blueprints
in same order for "P1–P6" price plans..$10 per set
Reverse Blueprints (mirror image) for "P1–P6" price plans ....$10 per set
1 Set of Deck Construction Details ....$14.95 each
Deck Construction Package ....**add $10 to Building Package price**
(includes 1 set of "P1–P6" plans, plus
1 set Standard Deck Construction Details)
1 Set of Gazebo Construction Details ....$14.95 each
Gazebo Construction Package ....**add $10 to Building Package price**
(includes 1 set of "P1–P6" plans, plus 1 set
Standard Gazebo Construction Details)

TO USE THE INDEX, refer to the design number listed in numerical order (a helpful page reference is also given). Note the price tier and refer to the House Blueprint Price Schedule above for the cost of one, four or eight sets of blueprints or the cost of a reproducible drawing. Additional prices are shown for identical and reverse blueprint sets, as well as a very useful Materials List for some of the plans. Also note in the Plan Index, those plans that have Deck Plans or Landscape Plans. Refer to the schedules above for prices of these plans. The letter "Y" identifies plans that are part of our Quote One® estimating service and those that offer Materials Lists. See page 198 for more information.

TO ORDER, Call toll free 1-800-521-6797 or 520-297-8200 for current pricing and availability prior to mailing the order form on page 205. FAX: 1-800-224-6699 or 520-544-3086.

PLAN INDEX

DESIGN	PRICE	PAGE	MATERIALS LIST	QUOTE ONE®	DECK	DECK PRICE	LANDSCAPE	LANDSCAPE PRICE	REGIONS
1404	A3	72	Y						
2439	A3	34	Y						
2493	A4	99	Y	Y					
2937	C3	193	Y	Y			OLA030	P3	12345678
3331	A3	11	Y	Y			OLA004	P3	123568
3360	L1	195	Y	Y			OLA008	P4	1234568
3361	L2	194	Y	Y			OLA031	P4	12345678

BEFORE YOU ORDER...

BEFORE FILLING OUT THE ORDER FORM, PLEASE CALL US ON OUR TOLL-FREE BLUEPRINT HOTLINE, YOU MAY WANT TO LEARN MORE ABOUT OUR SERVICES AND PRODUCTS. HERE'S SOME INFORMATION YOU WILL FIND HELPFUL.

OUR EXCHANGE POLICY

With the exception of reproducible plan orders, we will exchange your entire first order for an equal or greater number of blueprints within our plan collection within 90 days of the original order. The entire content of your original order must be returned before an exchange will be processed. Please call our customer service department for your return authorization number and shipping instructions. If the returned blueprints look used, redlined or copied, we will not honor your exchange. Fees for exchanging your blueprints are as follows: 20% of the amount of the original order...plus the difference in cost if exchanging for a design in a higher price bracket or less the difference in cost if exchanging for a design in a lower price bracket. **(Reproducible blueprints are not exchangeable or refundable.)** Please call for current postage and handling prices. Shipping and handling charges are not refundable.

ABOUT REVERSE BLUEPRINTS

Although lettering and dimensions will appear backward, reverses will be a useful aid if you decide to flop the plan. See Price Schedule and Plans Index for pricing.

REVISING, MODIFYING AND CUSTOMIZING PLANS

Like many homeowners who buy these plans, you and your builder, architect or engineer may want to make changes to them. We recommend purchase of a reproducible plan for any changes made by your builder, licensed architect or engineer. As set forth below, we cannot assume any responsibility for blueprints which have been changed, whether by you, your builder or by professionals selected by you or referred to you by us, because such individuals are outside our supervision and control.

ARCHITECTURAL AND ENGINEERING SEALS

Some cities and states are now requiring that a licensed architect or engineer review and "seal" a blueprint, or officially approve it, prior to construction due to concerns over energy costs, safety and other factors. Prior to application for a building permit or the start of actual construction, we strongly advise that you consult your local building official who can tell you if such a review is required.

ABOUT THE DESIGNS

The architects and designers whose work appears in this publication are among America's leading residential designers. Each plan was designed to meet the requirements of a nationally recognized model building code in effect at the time and place the plan was drawn. Because national building codes change from time to time, plans may not comply with any such code at the time they are sold to a customer. In addition, building officials may not accept these plans as final construction documents of record as the plans may need to be modified and additional drawings and details added to suit local conditions and requirements. We strongly advise that purchasers consult a licensed architect or engineer, and their local building official, before starting any construction related to these plans.

LOCAL BUILDING CODES AND ZONING REQUIREMENTS

At the time of creation, our plans are drawn to specifications published by the Building Officials and Code Administrators (BOCA) International, Inc.; the Southern Building Code Congress (SBCCI) International, Inc.; the International Conference of Building Officials (ICBO); or the Council of American Building Officials (CABO). Our plans are designed to meet or exceed national building standards. Because of the great differences in geography and climate throughout the United States and Canada, each state, county and municipality has its own building codes, zone requirements, ordinances and building regulations. Your plan may need to be modified to comply with local requirements regarding snow loads, energy codes, soil and seismic conditions and a wide range of other matters. In addition, you may need to obtain permits or inspections from local governments before and in the course of construction. Prior to using blueprints ordered from us, we strongly advise that you consult a licensed architect or engineer—and speak with your local building official—before applying for any permit or beginning construction. We authorize the use of our blueprints on the express condition that you strictly comply with all local building codes, zoning requirements and other applicable laws, regulations, ordinances and requirements. Notice: Plans for homes to be built in Nevada must be re-drawn by a Nevada-registered professional. Consult your building official for more information on this subject.

Have You Seen Our Newest Designs?

At least 50 of our latest creations are featured in each edition of our New Design Portfolio. You may have received a copy with your latest purchase by mail. If not, or if you purchased this book from a local retailer, just return the coupon below for your FREE copy. Make sure you consider the very latest of what Home Planners has to offer.

Yes! Please send my FREE copy of your latest New Design Portfolio.

Offer good to U.S. shipping address only.

Name _____

Address _____

City _____ State _____ Zip _____

HOME PLANNERS, LLC
Wholly owned by Hanley-Wood, LLC
3275 WEST INA ROAD, SUITE 110 • TUCSON, ARIZONA 85741

Order Form Key

HPT723

REGULAR OFFICE HOURS:
8:00 a.m.-10:00 p.m. EST, Monday-Friday,
10:00 a.m.-7:00 p.m. EST Sat & Sun.

If we receive your order by 3:00 p.m. EST, Monday-Friday, we'll process it and ship within **two business days**. When ordering by phone, please have your credit card ready. We'll also ask you for the Order Form Key Number at the bottom of the order form.

By FAX: Copy the Order Form on the next page and send it on our FAX line: 1-800-224-6699 or 520-544-3086.

Canadian Customers
Order Toll Free 1-877-223-6389

DISCLAIMER

The designers we work with have put substantial care and effort into the creation of their blueprints. However, because they cannot provide on-site consultation, supervision and control over actual construction, and because of the great variance in local building requirements, building practices and soil, seismic, weather and other conditions, WE CANNOT MAKE ANY WARRANTY, EXPRESS OR IMPLIED, WITH RESPECT TO THE CONTENT OR USE OF THE BLUEPRINTS, INCLUDING BUT NOT LIMITED TO ANY WARRANTY OF MERCHANTABILITY OR OF FITNESS FOR A PARTICULAR PURPOSE. **ITEMS, PRICES, TERMS AND CONDITIONS ARE SUBJECT TO CHANGE WITHOUT NOTICE. REPRODUCIBLE PLAN ORDERS MAY REQUIRE A CUSTOMER'S SIGNED RELEASE BEFORE SHIPPING.**

TERMS AND CONDITIONS

These designs are protected under the terms of United States Copyright Law and may not be copied or reproduced in any way, by any means, unless you have purchased Reproducibles which clearly indicate your right to copy or reproduce. We authorize the use of your chosen design as an aid in the construction of one single family home only. You may not use this design to build a second or multiple dwellings without purchasing another blueprint or blueprints or paying additional design fees.

HOW MANY BLUEPRINTS DO YOU NEED?

Although a standard building package may satisfy many states, cities and counties, some plans may require certain changes. For your convenience, we have developed a Reproducible plan which allows a local professional to modify and make up to 10 copies of your revised plan. As our plans are all copyright protected, with your purchase of the Reproducible, we will supply you with a Copyright release letter. The number of copies you may need, 1 for owner; 3 for builder; 2 for local building department and 1-3 sets for your mortgage lender.

ORDER TOLL FREE!
FOR INFORMATION ABOUT ANY OF OUR SERVICES OR TO ORDER CALL

1-800-521-6797
OR 520-297-8200
Browse our website:
www.eplans.com

BLUEPRINTS ARE NOT REFUNDABLE EXCHANGES ONLY

FOR CUSTOMER SERVICE,
CALL TOLL FREE **1-888-690-1116.**

HOME PLANNERS, LLC wholly owned by Hanley-Wood, LLC
3275 WEST INA ROAD, SUITE 110 • TUCSON, ARIZONA • 85741

THE BASIC BLUEPRINT PACKAGE
Rush me the following (please refer to the Plans Index and Price Schedule in this section):
___Set(s) of blueprints, plan number(s) _____ indicate foundation type _____ $_____
___Set(s) of reproducibles, plan number(s) _____ indicate foundation type _____ $_____
___Additional identical blueprints (standard or reverse) in same order @ $50 per set. $_____
___Reverse blueprints @ $50 fee per order. Right-reading reverse @ $165 surcharge $_____

IMPORTANT EXTRAS
Rush me the following:
___Materials List: $60 (Must be purchased with Blueprint set.) Add $10 for Schedule C4–L4 plans. $_____
___**Quote One®** Summary Cost Report @ $29.95 for one, $14.95 for each additional,
    for plans _____ $_____
    Building location: City _____ Zip Code _____
___**Quote One®** Materials Cost Report @ $120 Schedules P1–C3; $130 Schedules C4–L4,
    for plan_____ (Must be purchased with Blueprints set.) $_____
    Building location: City _____ Zip Code _____
___Specification Outlines @ $10 each. $_____
___Detail Sets @ $14.95 each; any two $22.95; any three $29.95; all four for $39.95 (save $19.85). $_____
    ❏ Plumbing ❏ Electrical ❏ Construction ❏ Mechanical
___Plan-A-Home® @ $29.95 each. $_____

DECK BLUEPRINTS
(Please refer to the Plans Index and Price Schedule in this section)
___Set(s) of Deck Plan _____. $_____
___Additional identical blueprints in same order @ $10 per set. $_____
___Reverse blueprints @ $10 fee per order. $_____
___Set of Standard Deck Details @ $14.95 per set. $_____
___Set of Complete Deck Construction Package (Best Buy!) Add $10 to Building Package
    Includes Custom Deck Plan _____ Plus Standard Deck Details

LANDSCAPE BLUEPRINTS
(Please refer to the Plans Index and Price Schedule in this section)
___Set(s) of Landscape Plan _____. $_____
___Additional identical blueprints in same order @ $10 per set. $_____
___Reverse blueprints @ $10 fee per order. $_____
Please indicate the appropriate region of the country for Plant & Material List.
(See map on page 200): Region _____

POSTAGE AND HANDLING	1–3 sets	4+ sets
Signature is required for all deliveries. **DELIVERY** No CODs (Requires street address—No P.O. Boxes)		
•Regular Service (Allow 7–10 business days delivery)	❏ $20.00	❏ $25.00
•Priority (Allow 4–5 business days delivery)	❏ $25.00	❏ $35.00
•Express (Allow 3 business days delivery)	❏ $35.00	❏ $45.00
OVERSEAS DELIVERY	fax, phone or mail for quote	

Note: All delivery times are from date Blueprint Package is shipped.

POSTAGE (From box above) $_____
SUBTOTAL $_____
SALES TAX (AZ & MI residents, please add appropriate state and local sales tax.) $_____
TOTAL (Subtotal and tax) $_____

YOUR ADDRESS (please print legibly)
Name _____

Street _____

City _____ State _____ Zip _____

Daytime telephone number (required) (_____) _____

FOR CREDIT CARD ORDERS ONLY
Credit card number _____ Exp. Date: (M/Y) _____
Check one ❏ Visa ❏ MasterCard ❏ Discover Card ❏ American Express

Order Form Key

Signature (required) _____ | HPT723 |

Please check appropriate box: ❏ Licensed Builder-Contractor ❏ Homeowner

☎ ORDER TOLL FREE!
1-800-521-6797 or 520-297-8200

BY FAX: Copy the order form above and send it on our FAXLINE: 1-800-224-6699 OR 1-520-544-3086

HELPFUL BOOKS & SOFTWARE

TO ORDER BY PHONE 1-800-322-6797

HOME PLANNERS WANTS YOUR BUILDING EXPERIENCE TO BE AS PLEASANT AND TROUBLE-FREE AS POSSIBLE.

That's why we've expanded our library of Do-It-Yourself titles to help you along. In addition to our beautiful plans books, we've added books to guide you through specific projects as well as the construction process. In fact, these are titles that will be as useful after your dream home is built as they are right now.

BIGGEST & BEST

1001 of our best-selling plans in one volume. 1,074 to 7,275 square feet. 704 pgs $12.95 1K1

ONE-STORY

450 designs for all lifestyles. 800 to 4,900 square feet. 384 pgs $9.95 OS

MORE ONE-STORY

475 superb one-level plans from 800 to 5,000 square feet. 448 pgs $9.95 MOS

TWO-STORY

443 designs for one-and-a-half and two stories. 1,500 to 6,000 square feet. 448 pgs $9.95 TS

VACATION

465 designs for recreation, retirement and leisure. 448 pgs $9.95 VSH

HILLSIDE

208 designs for split-levels, bi-levels, multi-levels and walkouts. 224 pgs $9.95 HH

FARMHOUSE

200 country designs from classic to contemporary by 7 winning designers. 224 pgs $8.95 FH

COUNTRY HOUSES

208 unique home plans that combine traditional style and modern livability. 224 pgs $9.95 CN

BUDGET-SMART

200 efficient plans from 7 top designers, that you can really afford to build! 224 pgs $8.95 BS

BARRIER FREE

Over 1,700 products and 51 plans for accessible living. 128 pgs $15.95 UH

ENCYCLOPEDIA

500 exceptional plans for all styles and budgets—the best book of its kind! 528 pgs $9.95 ENC

ENCYCLOPEDIA II

500 completely new plans. Spacious and stylish designs for every budget and taste. 352 pgs $9.95 E2

AFFORDABLE

Completely revised and updated, featuring 300 designs for modest budgets. 256 pgs $9.95 AF

VICTORIAN

NEW! 210 striking Victorian and Farmhouse designs from today's top designers. 224 pgs $15.95 VDH2

ESTATE

Dream big! Twenty-one designers showcase their biggest and best plans. 208 pgs $15.95 EDH

LUXURY

170 lavish designs, over 50% brand-new plans added to a most elegant collection. 192 pgs $14.95 LD2

EUROPEAN STYLES

200 homes with a unique flair of the Old World. 224 pgs $15.95 EURO

COUNTRY CLASSICS

Donald Gardner's 101 best Country and Traditional home plans. 192 pgs $17.95 DAG

WILLIAM POOLE

70 romantic house plans that capture the classic tradition of home design. 160 pgs $17.95 WEP

TRADITIONAL

85 timeless designs from the Design Traditions Library. 160 pgs $17.95 TRA

COTTAGES

25 fresh new designs that are as warm as a tropical breeze. A blend of the best aspects of many coastal styles. 64 pgs. $19.95 CTG

CLASSIC

Timeless, elegant designs that always feel like home. Gorgeous plans that are as flexible and up-to-date as their occupants. 240 pgs. $9.95 CS

CONTEMPORARY

The most complete and imaginative collection of contemporary designs available anywhere. 240 pgs. $9.95 CM

EASY-LIVING

200 efficient and sophisticated plans that are small in size, but big on livability. 224 pgs $8.95 EL

SOUTHERN

207 homes rich in Southern styling and comfort. 240 pgs $8.95 SH

SOUTHWESTERN

138 designs that capture the spirit of the Southwest. 144 pgs $10.95 SW

WESTERN

215 designs that capture the spirit and diversity of the Western lifestyle. 208 pgs $9.95 WH

NEIGHBORHOOD

170 designs with the feel of main street America. 192 pgs $12.95 TND

CRAFTSMAN

170 Home plans in the Craftsman and Bungalow style. 192 pgs $12.95 CC

COLONIAL HOUSES

181 Classic early American designs. 208 pgs $9.95 COL

DUPLEX & TOWNHOMES

Over 50 designs for multi-family living. 64 pgs $9.95 DTP

WATERFRONT

200 designs perfect for your waterside wonderland. 208 pgs $10.95 WF

206

PROJECT GUIDES

WINDOWS	STREET OF DREAMS	MOVE-UP	OUTDOOR	GARAGES	DECKS	HOME BUILDING	BOOK & CD-ROM

33 Discover the power of windows with over 160 designs featuring Pella's best. 192 pgs $9.95 WIN

34 Over 300 photos showcase 54 prestigious homes. 256 pgs $19.95 SOD

35 200 stylish designs for today's growing families from 9 hot designers. 224 pgs $8.95 MU

36 74 easy-to-build designs, lets you create and build your own backyard oasis. 128 pgs $7.95 YG

37 101 multi-use garages and outdoor structures to enhance any home. 96 pgs $7.95 GG

38 25 outstanding single-, double- and multi-level decks you can build. 112 pgs $7.95 DP

39 Everything you need to know to work with contractors and subcontractors. 212 pgs $14.95 HBP

40 Both the Home Planners Gold book and matching Windows™ CD-ROM with 3D floorplans. $24.95 HPGC Book only $12.95 HPG

LANDSCAPE DESIGNS

SOFTWARE	EASY-CARE	FRONT & BACK	BACKYARDS	BUYER'S GUIDE	FRAMING	BASIC WIRING	TILE

41 Home design made easy! View designs in 3D, take a virtual reality tour, add decorating details and more. $59.95 PLANSUITE

42 41 special landscapes designed for beauty and low maintenance. 160 pgs $14.95 ECL

43 The first book of do-it-yourself landscapes. 40 front, 15 backyards. 208 pgs $14.95 HL

44 40 designs focused solely on creating your own specially themed backyard oasis. 160 pgs $14.95 BYL

45 A comprehensive look at 2700 products for all aspects of landscaping & gardening. 128 pgs $19.95 LPBG

46 For those who want to take a more hands-on approach to their dream. 319 pgs $21.95 SRF

47 A straightforward guide to one of the most misunderstood systems in the home. 160 pgs $12.95 CBW

48 Every kind of tile for every kind of application. Includes tips on use, installation and repair. 176 pgs $12.95 CWT

BATHROOMS	KITCHENS	HOUSE CONTRACTING	VISUAL HANDBOOK	ROOFING	WINDOWS & DOORS	PATIOS & WALKS	TRIM & MOLDING

49 An innovative guide to organizing, remodeling and decorating your bathroom. 96 pgs $10.95 CDB

50 An imaginative guide to designing the perfect kitchen. Chock full of bright ideas to make your job easier. 176 pgs $16.95 CKI

51 Everything you need to know to act as your own general contractor, and save up to 25% off building costs. 134 pgs $14.95 SBC

52 A plain-talk guide to the construction process; financing to final walk-through, this book covers it all. 498 pgs $19.95 RVH

53 Information on the latest tools, materials and techniques for roof installation or repair. 80 pgs $7.95 CGR

54 Installation techniques and tips that make your project easier and more professional looking. 80 pgs $7.95 CGD

55 Clear step-by-step instructions take you from the basic design stages to the finished project. 80 pgs $7.95 CGW

56 Step-by-step instructions for installing baseboards, window and door casings and more. 80 pgs $7.95 CGT

Additional Books Order Form

To order your books, just check the box of the book numbered below and complete the coupon. We will process your order and ship it from our office within two business days. Send coupon and check (in U.S. funds).

YES! Please send me the books I've indicated:

❑ 1:IKI $12.95	❑ 20:TRA $17.95	❑ 39:HBP $14.95
❑ 2:OS $9.95	❑ 21:CTG $19.95	❑ 40:HPG $12.95
❑ 3:MOS $9.95	❑ 22:CS $9.95	❑ 40:HPGC $24.95
❑ 4:TS $9.95	❑ 23:CM $9.95	❑ 41:PLANSUITE .. $59.95
❑ 5:VSH $9.95	❑ 24:EL $8.95	❑ 42:ECL $14.95
❑ 6:HH $9.95	❑ 25:SH $8.95	❑ 43:HL $14.95
❑ 7:FH $8.95	❑ 26:SW $10.95	❑ 44:BYL $14.95
❑ 8:CN $9.95	❑ 27:WH $12.95	❑ 45:LPBG $19.95
❑ 9:BS $8.95	❑ 28:TND $12.95	❑ 46:SRF $21.95
❑ 10:UH $15.95	❑ 29:CC $12.95	❑ 47:CBW $12.95
❑ 11:ENC $9.95	❑ 30:COL $9.95	❑ 48:CWT $12.95
❑ 12:E2 .... $9.95	❑ 31:DTP $9.95	❑ 49:CDB $10.95
❑ 13:AF $9.95	❑ 32:WF $10.95	❑ 50:CKI $16.95
❑ 14:VDH2 .... $15.95	❑ 33:WIN $9.95	❑ 51:SBC $14.95
❑ 15:EDH $15.95	❑ 34:SOD $19.95	❑ 52:RVH $19.95
❑ 16:LD2 .... $14.95	❑ 35:MU $8.95	❑ 53:CGR $7.95
❑ 17:EURO $15.95	❑ 36:YG $7.95	❑ 54:CGD $7.95
❑ 18:DAG $17.95	❑ 37:GG $7.95	❑ 55:CGW $7.95
❑ 19:WEP $17.95	❑ 38:DP $7.95	❑ 56:CGT $7.95

Canadian Customers Order Toll Free 1-877-223-6389

Additional Books Subtotal (Please print) $ _____

ADD Postage and Handling (allow 4–6 weeks for delivery) $ 4.00

Sales Tax: (AZ & MI residents, add state and local sales tax.) $ _____

YOUR TOTAL (Subtotal, Postage/Handling, Tax) $ _____

YOUR ADDRESS (PLEASE PRINT)

Name _____

Street _____

City _____ State _____ Zip _____

Phone (_____) _____ — _____

YOUR PAYMENT

Check one: ❑ Check ❑ Visa ❑ MasterCard ❑ Discover ❑ American Express
Required credit card information:

Credit Card Number _____

Expiration Date (Month/Year) _____ / _____

Signature Required _____

Home Planners, LLC
Wholly owned by Hanley-Wood, LLC
® 3275 W. Ina Road, Suite 110, Dept. BK, Tucson, AZ 85741

HPT723

207

2103

Notes